MARCY,

MAY ALL
BE SAFE!

All THE BEST,

THE SHORTEST STRAW
SEARCH AND RESCUE IN THE HIGH SIERRA

DEAN ROSNAU

STEEP
STONE
GRADE

Printed in the United States of America.

Library of Congress Cataloging-in-Publication Data

Rosnau, Dean
    The Shortest Straw: a true accounting of Search and Rescue operations
in the eastern high Sierra Nevada by Dean Rosnau; illustrations by TJ
Russell.

ISBN: 978-1-49-990299-0

CONTENTS

Preface

Within the pages of this book I recount just a few of my experiences working as a Search and Rescue (SAR) professional over the course of my life. Though these stories are told from my personal perspective, the reality is that these types of incidents involve myriad people who selflessly donate countless hours of their time in the pursuit of saving lives. In every way SAR is a team effort.

Here in the United States, the Sheriff of each county is responsible for SAR response in a given situation. Most counties rely heavily on volunteers to provide these services, as the cost for paid teams would be prohibitive.

SAR team members come from all walks of life. Most teams are made up of people who simply love the outdoors and desire to serve their community in a unique and profound way.

Due to its close proximity to the urban areas of Southern California and the extensive number of visitors to the region, Mono County in the eastern high Sierra fields one of the busiest SAR teams in the nation. The team averages a call-out every nine days, year round.

Often, additional resources are needed to support larger scale searches or provide specific areas of expertise. Along with SAR teams from neighboring counties and domestic air resources, Mono County is blessed with assistance from all branches of the military. Not only do these men and women protect us from foreign threats, their unwavering courage saves countless lives within our borders every day.

I would personally like to recognize the professionalism of the men and women who make up the following resources, with whom I've been proud to serve:

• United States Marine Corps at the Mountain Warfare Training Center at Pickel Meadows, Mono County, California.

• Helicopter crews from the Naval Air Stations at Fallon, Nevada, Lemoore, California, and China Lake, California.

• Helicopter crews from the U.S Air Force at Mather Field, Sacramento, California.

• Helicopter crews from the U.S.D.A. Forest Service Hotshot Crew, Ship 525, Independence, California.

• Helicopter crews from the California Highway Patrol in Fresno, California.

• Helicopter crews from Yosemite National Park at Crane Flat.

Finally, it should be understood by every user of the outdoors that each SAR operation puts the lives of dedicated rescuers at risk. Come into the mountains with an attitude of self-reliance, come well prepared for the unexpected, and do everything in your power to mitigate the need to call for a rescue.

Should you ever need it, the best of the best will be on their way.

Acknowledgements

As a building contractor, I spent my career crafting stacks of wood into someone's dream home. It may have been my name on the contract, but to say that I built the place couldn't be further from the truth. It took a cadre of amazingly talented individuals to take a project from foundation to finish.

This is my first attempt at crafting something worthy of reading. Though I've always had a passion for writing, admittedly I'm not the sharpest knife in the drawer. There have been many individuals along the way to help me get this work into your hands. I would be remiss if I did not mention them here.

Not only did my late mentor, Rev. Luther Schwartzkopf encourage me to write, his passion for the outdoors and for making a difference in people's lives was infectious. His life embodied "service above self," and profoundly affected my own. I am forever grateful for his instilling in me the desire to live my dreams and finish strong. I'll see you again, dear friend.

In 2001, my family and I began serving alongside friends Clark and Melinda Vaughn at *For His Children*, an orphanage they founded in Quito, Ecuador. Their commitment to laying their lives down for the benefit of others has been a shining example of God's love for people. Their lives of service shaped our family in ways we never could have imagined. Not only did they give us vision for the future, while working alongside them we gained a daughter when we adopted 5 year-old Marina in 2009. Clark and Melinda's dedication to finishing what they started helped inspire me to stay focused on the keyboard, even when the mountains were calling.

I am forever in the debt of Bob and Pat Greene, and their daughter Tiffany, who allowed me to share the story of their beloved son and brother, Matthew Greene. Their courage and strength in the face of unspeakable tragedy and grief inspires me daily. Their contributions to this book are pure gold. Along with

Matthew's friends and colleagues, they have become family. I thank God for them all.

While in construction, I winnowed plenty of poor lumber over the years, choosing the best to achieve the finest end result. As I waded into the literary world, it was clear from the start that I was over my head in achieving anything worthy of a fine finished product. Renowned author Stephen King once said, "To write is human; to edit is divine." I am deeply grateful for my editor, Susan Barich, who not only helped craft my blathering into comprehensible thought, she walked beside me through memories that have at times been hard to bear. My twisted sense of humor could have driven her away. That she stuck with me is testament to her character and integrity. These pages are a shining example of her commitment to excellence.

By all accounts, I've lived an extraordinary life. For the rest of my days, I will be in debt to my amazing family: wife Leah, son Paden, and daughters Micah and Marina. They have all played a huge role in allowing me to pursue my passions, and subsequently, save some lives. The sacrifice of their time with me, sometimes not seeing me for days at a time, is why I have a story to tell. And time after time, they prayed me home, always expecting me to walk back through the door. I'll spend the rest of my life trying to give back what I've been given. Our unconditional love for each other is the best part of my life.

As certain as I am of all of the above, I am of this; God is good, all the time. He deserves all the glory.

INTRODUCTION

When I arrived in California as a 7 year old in 1969, I never dreamed that mountains would be in my future. It would not be long before the Sierra Nevada would capture my heart, and my life would change forever in profound ways.

Climbing became an obsession at a very early age, with the towering walls of Yosemite and the high country beyond as my dream. With every bit of air I got under my feet, that dream became my reality.

Climbing these peaks was one goal; living amongst them was another dream that seemed too grand to even comprehend. When I moved to the eastern high Sierra town of Mammoth Lakes in 1989, I considered myself the most blessed man on the planet. The high and wild places that I craved were now literally right outside my door.

Over the years, the mountains have been a diligent tutor. I've learned more life lessons while climbing peaks than in any other form of education. In the pages that follow you will see that many of those lessons have not been easy. Frankly, some have come with a terrible price. These astoundingly beautiful places that have brought me unfathomable joy, have tried to kill me countless times. But they are not malevolent. They are simply places that demand respect and a willingness to stay focused, obedient and humble.

Not only have the mountains become my home, but the friendships I've developed while playing in them have been priceless. Bonds that are formed while roped together, trusting each other with our lives and shaped through adversity, are as strong as the stone that united us. My gratitude for these relationships and deep respect for users of the outdoors made me want to give back to such an amazing group of people.

The world of alpine Search and Rescue (SAR) has proven to be a great way for me to do that. Not only do I get to sate my appetite for being in the wilderness, I've had the opportunity to use the skills I've gleaned over the years to help those who may not be having one of their better days.

Along with the joy of volunteering to do something fun and rewarding, SAR has been very demanding as well, both physically and emotionally. With that in mind, you are about to read some things that may prove disturbing to you. Though I've tried to use discretion in regards to describing some of these events of my life, I've also attempted to convey them in a manner that helps you, the reader, feel almost as if you were there. In doing that, there are a few instances where you will encounter some language and descriptive terms that you may find offensive. Again, in an attempt to bring you a glimpse of my world, I've tried to keep things as they happened. My apologies in advance.

I believe all of us are given certain talents and gifts that we can use to make the world in which we live a better place. Volunteerism has been one of the most rewarding aspects of my life. I'd encourage everyone to find your niche and bloom there. There is no greater joy than making a difference in someone's life ... especially that of a perfect stranger.

Finally, even if you are not the adventurous type and never spend any time in a wilderness environment, there are lessons in this book to be heeded. It is my prayer that as you read these pages, you would consider it a tutorial. Perhaps you won't be able to apply it to your own life, but you may know someone who would benefit greatly from the lessons I've learned from a lifetime in the mountains. I would consider it a great honor if you recommended this book to someone who may apply these things to their life of adventure. Saving lives has been the greatest honor of my life. If even one life is saved by the words in this book, I'd count that pure joy!

I believe God's guardian angels have been with me throughout my life. Some evidence of that is presented here in the pages that follow. Each day is a gift, and should be lived as if it were our last.

And may we never let a day go by without telling those in our life whom we love, just how much we love them.

Live your dreams . . . and finish strong!

Dean Rosnau
San Luis Obispo, California
March 2017

x

For Leah . . .

PROLOGUE

. . . on that day
all the springs of the great deep burst forth,
and the floodgates of the heavens
were open . . .

Genesis 7:11

January 2, 1997
3:05 p.m.
Mountain Gate Lodge, Walker Canyon

The Walker River was trying its level best to kill me. Water
that moments before might have been snow or ice raged
through my legs. I clung desperately to a cedar tree, pulling
myself into a small eddy at the tree's base. Floodwaters began
inundating the highway, forcing my fellow rescue-team members
farther and farther away. It became clear they would not get a
lifeline to me.

My boots were full of icy water and felt like anchors that
would take me straight down. Someone yelled, "Swim for it!" But I
simply could not get myself to venture from the relative safety of
the tree and further into the raging, debris-laden torrent without
a line to cling to. My heart sank at the looks of desperation and
hopelessness on my teammates' faces as they stared helplessly
from the road.

A large chunk of debris slammed into the tree I was clinging to. It lodged just above my hands, which were now painfully frozen from the incessant ice water. The debris created a dam, and a huge wave of water enveloped me as it roared past either side of the tree. My instincts told me to climb.

I reached up for the first branch, my hands like claws, unable to grasp. I hooked the first branch with the crook of my wrist, then the next branch with the other. Clawing my way, I scrambled out of the water.

Twelve feet away, I saw the young Marine, David, who was trapped against the wall of the house, holding on to another tree growing against the building. The desperate look on his face matched my own. Above the roar of the torrent, I yelled, "Climb that tree and get on the roof!" Without hesitation, he started up.

Once I was high enough in the tree to keep my feet out of the river, I became desperate for rest. Using one of the slings hanging from my harness, I tied myself off to the branches and slumped into a fetal position. I stuffed my hands down into my parka in hopes of getting some measure of warmth back into my frozen and aching fingers.

I could see that David had made it safely onto the roof. He fought against uncontrollable shivering brought on by intensely cold water and fear. For now, he was safe.

Looking across the river from my perch in the tree, I saw that the helicopter had finished hoisting out our four other rescue personnel and was now winching up the young family who had been trapped in their rental cabin when the flooding river jumped its banks earlier that morning. I could also see the rest of the rescue team who had been staged on the highway to assist, but were now being forced out of the area by the rapidly growing deluge. I was starting to feel very much alone.

Darkness was rapidly approaching, and I knew the chopper must be running low on fuel. Could they stay in the air long enough to retrieve both David and me?

With the family safely on the chopper, the ship flew off into the gathering darkness to take them to the evacuation center a few miles away. As it disappeared around the end of the canyon, I prayed it would return. Below me, the rising water was forcing me to climb higher into the tree.

David had scrambled up the roof, and was clinging to the rock chimney at the ridge. The first floor of the two-story house was now under water, and the entire building creaked and groaned. Suddenly, an adjacent house disintegrated with a tremendous explosion of snapping wood and breaking glass as the raging, muddy water washed it completely away in a matter of seconds.

Once again, overworked adrenaline glands flushed my system with raw energy. I was desperate for a solution and secretly hoped David had some sort of answer to our predicament. I called out to him above the roar of the water and waved him down to the edge of the roof nearest to me. As he approached, I saw by the look on his face that he wasn't going to be of much help. He had no gear with him, other than the life vest he was wearing over a wetsuit.

The tree I was in was twelve feet from the roof -- too far for me to make it to him without some rope. I yelled for him to see if he could climb down into a small tree between the rooftop he was on and the roof of an adjacent building that we had used as a platform for our rescue attempt earlier that day. If he could reach that rooftop, he could retrieve a section of rope we had left behind. Just twenty feet of rope would allow me to get out of my tree and onto the roof with him.

David eased his way to the edge of the roof, but one look at the swirling, icy death below forced him back. He yelled out to me, "I think I can get over to the other roof, but I don't think I can make it back!" I begged him to give it a try, but he was adamant that it didn't look good. He turned from me and went back up to the chimney. I slumped back into my fetal position trying to ward off the dread coursing through my veins.

My mind raced for a solution, and the thought of swimming for it plagued me. I didn't want any part of being in that river anymore. The entire tree shuddered as if it would topple over at any moment as debris slammed into it.

I needed an alternate plan, should the helicopter not return. Climbing higher into the tree to keep out of the rising water, I realized that I was high enough to reach out and grab a set of cables that ran past the tree and between power poles both up and downstream of my tree.

Being in the construction industry, I knew these low wires were television and phone lines, with virtually no voltage, and they were supported by a braided, steel cable.

I began to see a plan. I could reach out and clip one of my slings to the cable, release myself from the tree, then traverse the cable above the water to the downstream power pole, about fifty yards away. A few of my team members were only thirty feet from that pole.

My heart raced at the thought of a possible way out. But concern over the integrity of the cable, or where it was attached to the poles, or the poles themselves, made me doubt my plan. I knew the upstream pole had been subject to the raging water for the previous eight hours. It might be ready to go, and, if I added my weight, I could find myself in the water, hopelessly attached to hundreds of feet of cable.

Along with the uncertainty of the cable, if it did work and I got out, it did nothing to help David on the roof. Whether I could be of any help to him or not was in question, but I couldn't just leave him there to die.

He was standing on one of three remaining buildings. The other nine had disintegrated before our eyes over the course of the day. If the building immediately upstream from him went, the house he was on was going to take the full wrath of the force, and the trees would be his only hope. I decided that traversing the cable would be my last resort, should my tree begin to go down.

Darkness was falling, as the water rose closer to my feet. Another loud explosion of splintering wood caused me to whirl around, as a barn with two horses in it completely disintegrated. Helplessly, I watched in horror as the horses were washed to their deaths in a matter of seconds.

My body shivered uncontrollably as I began to resign myself to the same fate. As I hung from my harness, I closed my eyes, and my thoughts drifted to my wife, Leah, and the two kids, Paden and Micah. They were on their way home from a visit to Grandma's house. I was glad that at least they were unaware of my predicament. Oh, how desperately I wanted to be in their arms.

As thoughts of leaving them behind swept over me, I finally gave in, and tears flowed as I wept uncontrollably from deep within my soul. Picturing my own death in the waters raging beneath my feet brought on a fear like I'd never known before.

Over the roar of the river and the pouring rain, with teeth chattering, I cried out to God, praying that He would surround my family and me with His love. I wept as I was reminded of all the things I'd left undone that I knew God had put on my heart to accomplish for my family. I prayed that I would have another chance, but if death were to be my fate, that it would be over quickly. I asked Him to cover my family, then resigned myself to His will, completely broken and humbled by His awesome might.

My life's adventures had carried me to the brink of destruction before. I had wondered over the years if it were true that, just at the moment of one's death, your life flashed before your eyes. I had certainly used up my "nine lives" long before this present brush with death, not that those facts made me feel any more comfortable considering my predicament. But to say God had been faithful in sending His guardian angels with me throughout my life is a bit of an understatement.

Like so many times before, once again I was at the mercy of the God whom I'd come to know as advocate, comforter, friend, and a loving and almighty Savior.

CHAPTER 1

. . . for the Lord will go before you,
the God of Israel
will be your rear guard.

Isaiah 52:12

E ach of us is the product of our past. In some way, the
experiences of our youth shape us and become the
foundational pages of the life we come to know. From my earliest
recollections, I had an inherent zeal for adventure.

As a country boy growing up in rural eastern Missouri, my
world consisted of the acres and acres of woods that were just a
hop over our backyard fence. My best friend, Mark, and I were the
kings of our own patch of heaven, and we immersed ourselves in
adventure as the trees, sinkholes, ponds and creeks beckoned.

Oblivious to the turmoil taking place in our country after the
assassination of J.F.K. and the beginnings of war in Viet Nam, we
were off each day, bent on finding adventure at every turn. Most
of the time, adventure found us as we strayed blindly into harm's
way. Why little boys seem to find near disaster on a daily basis is
beyond me, but Mark and I were no exception. For us, near
disaster was half the fun. The other half was surviving to tell the
tale.

Summers brought extraordinary joy. Treasures abounded in
the slimy creatures and wriggling bugs we caught in the creek
that flowed deep in the heart of the woods. Cool pools provided

relief from the ever-present summer humidity, and we swung Tarzan-like across the water on clumps of branches gathered from weeping willow trees growing along the bank.

We often stayed out all day, and it was not uncommon for us to come in for dinner covered in purple mulberry juice. During those balmy summer days, we returned with a host of ticks, chiggers, and leeches clinging to our bodies and had to endure the pain of "vermin removal" and the sting of rubbing alcohol. My parents would have been smart to buy stock in Calamine lotion, for I regularly sported a stunning pink glow from being slathered in the stuff to combat my bouts of poison-ivy rash.

Each season flowed into the next, as the scars and bruises of previous near brushes with death were covered by new ones. Little did I know that this pattern of near destruction would follow me through my adolescence and into adulthood. As the summer of 1968 rolled around, an event took place that would become a metaphor for the life that I've known.

At seven years old, there wasn't anything I was going to let my older brother do that I could not, which included riding his new bike all the way down our steep street. Stealthily, I waited until he had abandoned the bike in the front yard, then climbed aboard and pedaled for the top of the hill.

I couldn't sit on the seat; my feet would not reach the pedals sitting down, so I straddled the center bar as best as I could. The handlebars were as wide as my arms could stretch, but I was determined to succeed.

At the top of the hill I stopped to catch my breath. Looking down, I considered chickening out; it looked a lot steeper from high on this tall bike. But my brother had done it, so I must, too. I pointed the bike downhill and jumped aboard.

As we gained speed, I got up on the seat and, with legs dangling above the pedals, hollered my way down the hill. Tears streaked from my eyes as the wind blew into my face. I was on top of the world.

As I approached our house I decided I would take the bike right into the front yard, then go in and announce my triumph.

As I began to make the turn from the street into our driveway, my brother came out of the front door of the house and saw me on his bike. Distracted by his sudden appearance, I misjudged the turn and the speed of the bike and crashed headlong into the gas-lamp post that stood at the front corner of our driveway. A tremendous roar filled my head, and in an instant the bike and I landed in a heap in the front yard.

The next thing I knew, Mom was at my side. Blood poured from my mouth. We were off to the hospital.

On our way home my head screamed in pain, my mouth was packed with gauze, and stitches held together my lips and gums. My face was brutally swollen, and Mom wept at the sight. She looked over at my pitiful self.

"Honest to goodness, Dean, I think God's guardian angels must draw straws to see which of them has to go with you every day!"

I'm sure, from that moment on, God knew the paths that I would travel. Fortunately for me, He must have kept that information close to His vest, so as not to produce dissension in the ranks of those angels who, over the years, would have the misfortune of drawing the shortest straw.

In the early summer of 1969, a new chapter of adventures began in my life. My parents, having both lived their lives in the Midwest to this point, had grown weary of the long, cold winters, and yearned for sunnier climes.

With their sights set on Southern California, they packed up our belongings and their four children and headed west. This meant my finding a new batch of friends and a change of landscape that offered legions of adventure possibilities. It didn't take me long to find both.

When I met Wayne, it was clear from the start he was up for as much adventure as I could dish out. Not long after we met, we installed a rope swing on a large oak tree growing from a hillside a few miles from home. We spent many days pushing the arc of our swings to greater and greater heights.

When Wayne came flying off the rope, landed square on his head and was taken straight into the hospital, we were banned from the rope swing. Fortunately, Wayne had only suffered a bad concussion.

The end of one adventure only meant the start of another. And so it was that, not long after Wayne's world-record flight and survival, we set out for our next source of entertainment. Having been banned from all things above the ground, it was only logical to pursue things under the ground.

This seemed particularly brazen considering we had just survived the Sylmar earthquake in February of 1971, which shook our neck of the woods with a 6.9 temblor. I recall running out of the house early that morning with my family, only to discover the pavement of the street rolling like swells on the sea. Why two kids who had been terrified of the quakes would venture underground not long thereafter is beyond me now, but it seemed like just another perfect adventure at the time.

Near the base of the hills where our rope swing had been, a large flood control channel diverted run-off water into a huge underground pipe. The entrance of the pipe was about five feet wide and was blocked by a hinged, steel grate. The grate was there for a two-fold purpose: number one, to strain out debris from entering the pipe; and number two, to keep out curious kids like us. It failed at the latter.

Using branches that the grate had snagged, Wayne and I pried it up just enough to brace it open and crawl in. Once inside, we discovered that the pipe was in fact about eight feet in diameter. We walked down the pipe, deeper and deeper into the inky blackness and farther and farther from the light at the entrance.

About every hundred yards, a manhole cover at the ceiling of the pipe allowed tiny shafts of light to enter through the two holes in the steel lid. The "thump-thump" of vehicle wheels echoed through the pipe as cars drove over the manholes.

After a few hundred yards, the blackness got the best of our nerves, and we ran back to the entrance. We agreed that the pipe needed further exploration and vowed to return with flashlights in hand.

As we walked the two miles back home, we counted manhole covers. We determined that the pipe went well beyond our homes, but where it ended was a mystery, and it must be solved.

We returned the next day, not with flashlights, but with six road flares we had liberated from Wayne's garage. We crawled into the pipe, popped the first flare and descended into the unknown, eager to see where the pipe led. We counted manhole covers in an attempt to gauge where we were under the roadway as we went.

The floor of the pipe ran with slimy, green water about an inch deep, and we soon found out that stepping into the ooze was a quick way to end up on our backsides. We stayed to the side as best we could, walking on the slight camber of the pipe. As we descended, the small point of light at the entrance shrank to a speck. Soon, it was completely out of sight.

Before long, we were on our third flare, with three to go. We continued down nervously, hoping we would have enough flares to reach the end.

Well into the fifth flare, the pipe took a prominent turn to the left and reduced in size by a few feet. We could still easily walk standing upright, but it became harder to stay high enough on the pipe to keep our feet out of the muck.

Not long after making the turn, we saw a tiny speck of light. Now into our last flare, we were getting anxious, so we picked up our pace. Close to the end of the pipe, the light flooded in just as our last flare died. We felt like heroes, having grabbed the exact number of flares needed to traverse the pipe.

As we reached the end of the pipe, we could only stare in

disbelief. The tunnel had taken us all the way to the San José Creek, a large concrete flood control channel a full mile beyond our homes. We had walked underground for over three miles!

Suddenly, amidst our glee, a realization hit us. It was a twenty-foot drop from the end of the pipe to the concrete river channel below. And it was a good eight feet up to the chain link fence at the top of the channel. Our only way out was back through the pipe.

Facing back into the pitch blackness of the pipe produced a strain on my bladder like I'd never felt before. The thought of groping our way through miles of darkness seemed impossible. Before we could let the terror take hold, we strode headlong into the void.

We pushed on with our hands straight out in front of us. The thought of suddenly touching something menacing was terrifying, and we walked as fast as possible. We constantly slipped and fell into the green muck, which stank like a swamp. We reached the bend and continued on.

Just getting to the bend took forever, and going the other way we had been on our fifth flare at that point. We had a long way to go. We thought of trying to find a stick that we could push out the small hole in a manhole cover in hopes of alerting a car. But finding a stick meant groping in the slime, not to mention being found out by the parents. We kept moving. We'd fallen down so many times that the green ooze didn't bother us anymore. We just wanted out.

Finally, after what seemed like an eternity, we saw the small speck of light from our entry grate in the distance. Our hearts raced as we drew closer and closer. Our eyes played tricks on us, with each of us thinking that the light had disappeared momentarily. We quickened our pace, and finally got close enough to be able to see again.

As we approached the grate at the entrance, we looked each other over and laughed with nervous delight. Both of us were covered from head to toe with green, mossy, stinky ooze. We crawled out from under the propped open grate and up to the bank of the drainage channel. Sitting in the sunshine, staring at the entrance to the pipe, we felt as if we had achieved one of the truly great conquests of our time.

As the thought of our triumph healed our shattered nerves, it didn't take long before we were scheming once again to up the ante.

We thought of taping flashlights on our bikes and riding down the pipe, but we realized we could never keep our tires out of the muck, which would mean a lot of crashes and a good sliming. We headed down the road towards home, looking like two small Martians, but feeling like kings. By the time we reached home, we had it figured out. We would attempt to descend the pipe -- on a go-kart.

The design of our kart would be critical. Our first thought was to keep out of the slime; the wheels had to be far enough apart to stay clear of the water. Secondly, there had to be room for both of us at the same time, and we needed some lights strapped on the front. Lastly, we needed wheels that would allow for as much speed as possible, since the pipe wasn't steep enough to generate much velocity.

With tools procured from my father's garage and lumber salvaged from along the railways nearby, we constructed our frame utilizing the classic rope steering system.

We enlisted the help of Wayne's brother to find decent wheels and pipe for our axles. Our brakes would be the soles of our shoes. Within a few days we had a first-rate coaster kart that proved its worth going full steam down our block. It was time to head back to the pipe.

We managed to lift a section of chain-link fence high enough to squeeze the kart underneath and propped up the grate at the pipe entrance high enough to get the kart inside. How we managed all of this without being spotted by a wary adult is beyond me, but soon we were taping our flashlights to the front of our craft and preparing for our maiden voyage. We flipped a coin, with Wayne winning the right to be the driver, which meant I would be giving a mighty running push before jumping aboard.

With lights switched on and Wayne at the ready, I gave the kart a push, all the while trying to run off to the side to stay out of the water. I jumped aboard and we were on our way. The kart picked up speed as we whooped and hollered our way down into the darkness.

As we gained speed, Wayne swerved the kart back and forth up the side of the pipe. We whooped even louder, oblivious to the spray of the muck that came off the wheels as we swung from one side to the other.

Suddenly, there was a tremendous bang, and both Wayne and I flew head first in front of the kart. We landed in a heap in the slimy water, banging heads, knees and elbows into the hard concrete. As we slid to a stop, the pipe grew dark and quiet.

With the one flashlight that survived the crash, we examined the wreckage. The kart was lying upside down, with the entire front axle sheered off and one wheel completely shattered. After a few minutes of investigation, we realized what had happened.

Wayne had been swerving the kart back and forth on the walls of the pipe, and in our glee, we never considered the rungs of steel re-bar that served as steps under each manhole. We had struck the lowest rung with such force that it sheered one side of the steel bar from the concrete. Our kart fared far worse.

Dejected that we had only made it a few hundred yards down the pipe, we dragged our wreckage back to the entrance.

What we needed were slightly narrower axles, which would mean more soakings from the green muck, but less chance of hitting the rungs. We pried off the axles and headed home to re-design our craft.

After coming up with a new wheel and reworking the axle, we were ready for another shot. This time, we were far more prepared for the challenge. We brought a few tools and banged the axles back on. We taped on two additional flashlights, giving us four headlights, the better to spot the rungs. We brought kneepads and wore long sleeve shirts. We donned motorcycle helmets "borrowed" from Wayne's brother. Our final pieces of gear were scuba masks to keep the green slime out of our eyes.

Looking like a couple of escapees from an insane asylum, we were ready for another shot. It was a given that I was driving this time. Wayne pushed like a madman, and once again we were off.

With the additional lighting it was easy to spot the rungs as we made our way faster and faster down the tube. I swung the kart back and forth, producing a wave of muck with each pull of the rope. We were having such fun that we didn't even mind having to spit out the foul water.

We were headed for a complete passage and nothing was going to ruin that now. Within minutes, we were at the bend. The kart road high up the wall as we rounded the curve. We hollered with glee having made the turn at full speed.

Soon we were able to see the proverbial light at the end of the tunnel, and we were closing in on it fast. We hadn't discussed stopping or when we would begin to apply our personal braking system. By the time we tried to go into braking mode, we were so slimed that our shoes were virtually useless in slowing us down. The circle of light at the end of the tunnel was growing rapidly, and it was time to end this ride.

About a hundred yards from the light, it became obvious we weren't going to be able to stop the kart. Wayne bailed off the back and I pitched off the side, the rear wheel running me over. Together, we slid to a halt in the middle of the ooze and watched in disbelief as the kart disappeared out the end of the pipe.

Covered in a thick layer of green nastiness, we walked to the edge of the pipe and stared down at our shattered kart. It was lying in a heap of twisted boards, shattered wheels and scattered batteries. We looked at each other, then back into the inky black pipe. Resigned, we began the long walk back once again.

But this time, we were more confident. We had walked it in the dark once before, so we could do it again. And now we had ridden the length of the pipe with fearless abandon. To us, the pipe had been tamed. We'd lost our kart, but not before we did what we had set out to do.

We exited the pipe, green from head to toe, and proudly walked home in our motorcycle helmets and scuba masks, certain that Evel Kneivel had nothing on us.

A few months after our victorious trip down the pipe, another classmate of ours was severely burned when the gasoline he was using to clean his bicycle ignited, burning him over most of his body. Within a few days, he died of his injuries. Mom took me to his funeral. Seeing him in his coffin is a memory I will never forget. It made me realize that our actions could have serious consequences. I thought of our trip down the pipe, and how easy it would have been for one or both of us to have died down in the darkness. The death of my friend tempered my quest for the extreme, if only for a short time.

CHAPTER 2

Humble yourselves, therefore, under God's mighty hand,
that He may lift you up in due time.
Cast all your anxiety on Him
because He cares for you.

1 Peter 5:6-7

The unmistakable smell of incense cedar wafted on the warm summer breeze as my lungs gasped for air. We had left Yosemite Valley hours earlier from the trailhead at Happy Isles, made our way up the hundreds of steps of the famous Mist Trail past Vernal and Nevada Falls, and were now a mere 800 feet below our intended goal: the summit of Half Dome.

Our nation was caught up in the turmoil that was Watergate, but here, in this place, I might as well have been on the moon. I was oblivious to anything but what my eyes beheld. My whole world came down to that last 800 feet of granite. Nothing else mattered.

Within a few heart-pumping minutes, I'd scampered up the Park Service cables and stood atop the most awe-inspiring summit I could ever imagine. I'd been on God's green earth now for all of eleven years, had seen my share of adventure for a young life, but never had I dreamed of such a thrill. Something stirred deep within my being on that lofty precipice. Suddenly I saw the towering granite walls of Yosemite in a different light. A yearning like I'd never experienced before instilled in me a desire to visit the lofty heights of this place and beyond. I couldn't know it then, but on that hot August day in 1972, my life changed forever. Half Dome would be my touchstone.

Back in Yosemite Valley, I found myself drawn to the small Mountain Shop in Curry Village. This little store catered to a subculture of human beings the likes of which I had never seen. My parents would call them hippies, with their long hair, scraggly beards, and paisley-printed clothes. These shaggy-looking ragamuffins, somehow, some way, knew how to scale the towering walls of Yosemite, and I desperately wanted into their world.

Later that week, we took a group bike ride through the valley to the base of Bridalveil Falls. In the late summer heat, the falls were but a trickle. Along with others from our group, I scrambled up the boulder-strewn riverbed toward the base of the falls. As we approached the water-polished rock, I suddenly heard a cry for help. Rounding a large boulder of nearly eighty feet in height, we came across a ghastly scene. Lying in a shallow pool of water was the shattered body of a man, covered in blood. Another man was doing what he could to help. He spotted us and shouted for us to go get help.

I dashed down the boulders, heading for the path where we had left our bikes and where others were gathered to photograph the falls. Reaching a small group of people, I managed to explain between gasps of breath that help was needed right away. Calmly, a man walked down the trail to alert the rangers. I couldn't believe he was going so slowly when help was desperately needed. I ran past him and on down to the parking lot where I found a ranger.

Minutes later, the rescue team arrived, and I guided them back to the location. Days later, we learned that the injured man had not survived. I did not know it then, but years later I would relive this event in many fashions, over and over again.

Leaving Yosemite that week to head home on the outskirts of Los Angeles was, for me, akin to the Israelites heading back to Egypt from the Promised Land.

Later that fall, when my parents announced we were heading out to visit my great Aunt Elsie and Uncle Art, I was beside myself with glee. Previous trips to their house had been just another day trip to the high desert of Southern California to hang out with old people. With my newfound passion for all things granite or otherwise, visiting Art and Elsie's home in a place called Joshua Tree would take on a whole new meaning.

Joshua Tree National Park is a climber's mecca. Though I had not yet obtained the skills of a true rock climber, I scrambled around the huge boulders with fearless abandon. The scrapes and bruises that were part of the process were a badge of courage for me and learning this sport became an obsession. I immersed myself in books on the subject. *Mountaineering; The Freedom of the Hills* became my bible.

Annual trips to Yosemite with my church youth group added fire to the passion I had for all things vertical. Going back to the Mountain Shop was a sort of groupie pilgrimage. I'd hang out front and watch my heroes wander in and out with their torn clothing and shredded hands. I aspired to the heights they had achieved. Somehow, some way, I had to own this dream.

In 1975 I entered high school. My desires to become a climber had fallen on deaf ears with my parents; something about a history of hurting myself was their reasoning. One day that fall, I told my mom I was planning a report for one of my classes on the subject of rock climbing. I asked if she would take me to a local climbing shop to do a little research. The shop loaned me gear that I could use for my oral report. Just touching those few small tools shifted my desire into overdrive. Again, I asked my parents to let me take a climbing class, to no avail.

A few weeks later I did the only thing a completely obsessed fourteen year old had left to do; I rode my bike to the climbing shop my Mom had taken me to, and secretly signed up for the class. This class was held out in Joshua Tree. I was the only kid amongst ten adults, and I out-climbed them all. The instructor dubbed me a natural and encouraged me to pursue the sport. At this point, only incarceration could have kept me away.

For the next four years, my entire high school life, I carefully laid down a smokescreen of fibs and outright lies to keep my secret life from my parents. By graduation I was certain of two things: college was out, and Joshua Tree, Tahquitz and Yosemite Valley were all that mattered.

The summer of 1979 proved the best days of my young life. Living out of my truck and tent, eating out of a can, and hanging in a harness day after blissful day was the culmination of a nearly decade-long quest. Late that summer I climbed my first "big wall" in Yosemite, the towering Prow route on Washington's Column. Though not on the scale of Half Dome or El Capitan, my time on the Prow would be the harbinger of things to come and would cement climbing as a part of my life forever.

Every aspect of my life now revolved around climbing. If I couldn't afford the gas money to get to the rocks, I'd bum rides. If I couldn't afford the food, I'd do without. If the weather were poor, I'd read climbing books. And if a job got in the way of a good trip, I'd quit. Poverty was tolerable if climbing was the option.

In the late spring of 1983, I found myself with a couple weeks of time on my hands, and a deep yearning for Yosemite Valley. Loading my truck with gear, I headed north out of Los Angeles. I had no partner lined up but hoped to run into friends once I arrived. Unbeknownst to me, what lay ahead would be yet another brush with death that would change my life forever.

CHAPTER 3

... even though I enter the valley of death,
I will fear no evil,
for You are with me...

Psalm 23:4

I rolled into Camp 4, Yosemite's infamous climber's camp, on June 1st, 1983. As I had expected, a number of friends were there, though all were paired up with climbing partners. Initially discouraged, I quickly met up with an odd looking British chap by the name of Ian. He had been climbing about ten years and was on his first trip to Yosemite. I liked Ian immediately, though it was clear that bathing did not rate high on his priority list. We sealed our plans around the campfire that night and swapped tales of climbing adventures.

For the next week Ian allowed me to be his guide, directing him to some of the classic climbs I had done over the years. His quick wit and irrepressible accent of proper English overshadowed his near toxic aversion to personal hygiene. I was disappointed when, after a week of nonstop climbing on Yosemite's incomparable granite, Ian's appointed day to "jump the pond" had arrived. Only my nostrils were pleased.

I had another week to go in the Valley with high hopes of getting in plenty more climbs, but after a few days of partner hunting I was getting discouraged. I wandered over to the Mountain Shop where, years earlier, I had only the nerve to stand outside and watch the climbers go in and out. Now, I felt I belonged.

In the shop, I overheard a group of young guys asking one of the store employees about route information on climbing the Lost Arrow Spire. I eagerly waded into the conversation, hoping to weasel my way in to this party of climbers.

Tagging along with them back to the campground, I discovered that they were a group of five guys from Colorado. They had just arrived in the Valley and had come to climb the Lost Arrow. I suggested that if I joined them we would be three parties of two, and certainly more efficient than what they had planned. They agreed, and we sat around the fire that night laying out plans for the next day.

The Lost Arrow Spire is a truly unique feature in Yosemite Valley that most visitors completely miss. This 250 foot-tall tower of granite juts out from the valley rim just east of upper Yosemite Falls. It looks much like your thumb does in relation to your hand. Climbing on the Spire isn't overly difficult.

The attraction for climbers is the location, which is sublime, and the exposure, which is as steep as it gets. Between the nearly 2,000-foot drop and the close proximity to booming Yosemite Falls, the Spire is an adventurer's dream. But what really attracts climbers to this famous spire isn't the way up; it's the way off.

The Tyrolean Traverse is a climbing technique for crossing large voids or gaps between two fixed points, and the traverse off the Lost Arrow is the most famous Tyrolean Traverse on the planet. Here's how climbing the Arrow and the traverse works.

The first requirement is the four-and-a-half-mile hike up the Yosemite Falls trail, across the creek above the falls, then over to the rim of the Valley, itself. At a point directly across from the tip of the Spire, two 165 foot-long ropes are tied together, and one end is secured to a large tree on the canyon rim. You then rappel down this fixed rope approximately 280 feet to "the Notch," a decent-sized ledge where the Spire juts out from the wall.

The end of the rappel line is then clipped to the harness of one of the climbers in the party. The climbers ascend the route, which is located on the Valley side of the Spire, utilizing a separate climbing rope, all the while trailing the rappel line. Upon reaching the summit of the Spire, which is about the size of the hood on your grandma's Buick, the end of the trailed line is passed through the permanent anchor in the summit, and the slack is hauled up. The rope is then pulled tight between the top of the Spire and the tree on the rim of the Valley, and a knot is tied at the anchor point and secured. Now, there is a single line between the climbers and the tree on the rim, a distance of about eighty feet.

The slack end of the rope on the Spire is tied to the harness of the "guinea pig," the first climber to go across. The "pig" then clips into the line with a carabiner, an aluminum snap link, at his waist, along with a second carabiner for additional safety.

Because the canyon rim is about forty feet higher than the Spire, two mechanical ascenders are fixed to the rope and attached to one's harness. These devices use a toothed cam to grab the rope in a downward pull, but freely slide up the rope. Along with small stirrups or "aiders" attached to one's feet, ascenders allow a climber to quickly ascend a fixed rope. The climber then hauls himself across on the rope and up the steady incline.

Once the pig is across, the climber on the Spire unties the knot where the line was clipped to the anchor. Now there is simply a looped rope going through the anchor with no knots. The pig then hauls in all of the slack and ties that end to the tree. The second climber simply follows in the same manner as the pig. Once across, one end of the rope is untied from the tree and allowed to drop down off the wall and across to the Spire. Then the rope is hauled back through the anchor on the Spire and retrieved.

The next morning dawned bright and beautiful, and the six of us were up early. With gear, food and water packed, we hit the trail. I had known these guys only a few short hours, but, based on our conversation the night before, I was confident that they were experienced enough to handle the Lost Arrow. I continued to size them up as we made our way up the steep path.

Mike and Stu were the clear leaders of this bunch. They had climbed in Yosemite before and, though young, were obviously experienced. Both of them had brought their girlfriends along on this trip, though the reason why escaped me as the young men seemed to ignore them. The girls wished us well as we left the campsite and said they'd try to watch us from the Valley.

Kelly and Kyle were brothers. They were fairly new to the sport but seemed eager to do as much as possible while in Yosemite. They were regular partners back in Colorado and had spent a fair amount of time climbing near their home in Boulder. The Lost Arrow would be their first Yosemite route. I was concerned as to how they would fair with the considerable exposure, as they had stated that they had not climbed anything much higher than a few hundred feet. But they seemed highly motivated.

Carl was the youngest of the bunch at just eighteen. He had started climbing the summer before and had little experience. Stu had given him a crash course in using the ascenders around our campfire the night before. What he lacked in experience, he made up for in physical fitness; the guy was a gym rat, and it showed. Carl would be my partner for the day.

At about the three-mile mark on the trail, the Lost Arrow came into a wonderful profile view. We stopped to take a few pictures and enjoy some food while absorbing the incomparable scene of the roaring Yosemite Falls. Swollen with spring run-off, the fall was in full glory. A cool breeze brought a chill that motivated us to get back to hiking. We were all dressed in shorts and t-shirts, and I secretly wondered if I should have brought extra clothes. But it was still early, and the Valley should be warming up with every hour that went by.

After a couple hours of hiking we crossed the bridge over the creek above the falls and made our way off trail towards the Valley rim. A cool breeze blew out of the north. It made us all a bit uncomfortable. However, the Spire was below the rim and on a south-facing wall. We were sure we would soon be baking in the warm sun.

With the ropes fixed to the tree, we made our way down to the Notch. Carl struggled for a time at the knot where the two rappel lines were joined halfway down. At this point, ascenders are required to attach oneself to the line. Then the knot could be safely passed around the rappel device on Carl's harness. From below, we were able to talk him though the process, and soon he joined us at the Notch.

Mike was already climbing by the time I reached the Notch. He and Stu were using a double-rope system. Climbers will sometimes use a two-rope system when the route tends to wander around rather than ascend in a straight line. The second rope helps eliminate rope drag, or tension, caused by the rope being clipped through protection pieces that are not in a vertical line.

I knew the night before that they had planned to use the system and told them that, based on the guidebook information, as well as what we learned from the Mountain Shop employee, I didn't think the double rope was necessary. Mike and Stu wanted to stick to their normal routine. This was the way they were used to climbing.

To our dismay, the Notch was not immune to the cool breeze that we'd encountered on the rim; in fact, the wind seemed to have picked up. Mike hollered down that he was quite warm with the exertion of climbing, which made us all eager to get moving. As soon as Mike was at the top of the first pitch, Stu started up, with the trailing fixed line attached to his harness.

The first move off the Notch and out onto the Spire is exhilarating, and as Stu stepped out on to the exposed face of the route, he let out a whoop that made even the roar of the falls seem quiet. Right on his heels was Kelly, with Kyle as his belayer.

It was fortunate that the Notch is as big and reasonably flat as it is, since Carl and I had resorted to jumping jacks and push-ups to try to stay warm. We were in an honest to goodness wind now, and it was getting downright uncomfortable. Occasional gusts brought a slight dousing of spray from the nearby falls, which raged down the wall just 150 yards away. Getting only the slightest bit wet added to the misery.

Up on the route, Kelly struggled. Stu yelled down direction and encouragement to him. The three of us on the ledge were helpless to assist, since we could not see any of the climbers from our position. For nearly thirty minutes, Kyle had not paid out any rope, which meant Kelly was having a hard time. The wind was blowing in earnest now, and communicating with the guys above was difficult. We could not hear anything from Mike, and Stu's words were barely audible. Kelly was working hard and was not in the mood to relay anything from the guys above him.

Almost as if a switch had been flipped, clouds poured over the rim of the Valley just above the Falls. These were not the high, wispy-type things way up in the atmosphere. These clouds literally spilled over the rim like a grey fog, pushed along by an ever-increasing wind.

I took over the belay from Kyle so he could move around a bit to get his blood flowing. Kelly had been quiet for quite some time when, all of a sudden, he tried to communicate with Stu, above him. As we strained to hear the guys above, the clouds rapidly streamed across the blue sky. At the rate they were moving, it wouldn't be long before they blocked out the sun's rays.

The bouts of spray from the falls became more frequent as the wind picked up, and the three of us began talking about abandoning the climb. Had Stu not taken the fixed line with him, I'm certain two of us would have headed up the wall already.

Before we could suggest it, Kelly yelled that he was coming down and that Mike and Stu were setting up to rappel back down as well. I tightened the rope on Kelly and lowered him as he cleaned gear out of the crack. Within a few minutes he was back on the ledge with us. He said that Stu had yelled down that Mike was getting soaked at the start of the second pitch, which wraps around the Spire and is more prone to the mist from the falls.

Within minutes of Kelly making it back to the Notch, a light rain began to fall as the clouds thickened. We huddled against the wall of the Spire to gain as much protection as possible from both the rain and the gusts of wind, which brought a stinging spray from the waterfall.

To a man, we were underdressed for the weather. Not one of us had anticipated these conditions in the second week of June. We had made the rookie mistake of not checking the weather report prior to heading into such a committed and exposed position.

The wind howled now. The sound made any communication with Stu and Mike impossible. We knew they were dealing with setting up an anchor from which they could rappel down to us. Suddenly I was thankful for the double rope system they had employed, as it allowed them to make it back to the Notch in one rappel, thereby speeding up their arrival. We had been trying to yell to Stu to let the trail line loose, so that we could begin ascending the line to get out. We kept looking upwards in hopes of seeing the rope swinging down from above, but it never came.

The clouds overtook the direct sunshine, and the temperature plunged. The four of us were now crouched in a tight huddle of shivering muscles and chattering teeth. Above us, Mike and Stu were fairing much worse. They were fully exposed to the wind, rain and spray, and they were quickly sinking into a hypothermic state as they readied the ropes for their descent.

I'd been thinking about hypothermia for well over an hour. I had taught classes on the subject in the past, and was now getting my own crash course in how it affected the body. Hypothermia occurs when your body loses heat faster than it can produce heat, causing a dangerously low body temperature. Normal body temperature is around 98.6 degrees Fahrenheit. Hypothermia occurs as your body temperature passes below 95 degrees Fahrenheit.

Shivering is the body's response to the initial effects of the cold. Our muscles contract in an attempt to create warmth through movement. As the body continues to cool, blood vessels in the extremities constrict, slowing blood flow to the hands and feet in order to keep more blood in the core to protect vital organs. The core temperature only has to drop one degree for serious problems to begin. Eventually, the brain starts to suffer, causing a stupor that produces slow movement, poor judgment, and, eventually, a desire to lie down and go to sleep. Being wet and exposed to the wind magnifies the problem ten-fold.

We were now being drenched by a light but steady rain, and our teeth produced a collective staccato of chattering. After what seemed like hours, Stu and Mike swung around the corner of the Spire and onto the ledge. They had managed to rappel simultaneously, one down each of the two ropes that were tied together and looped through the anchor they had set. We jumped out of our crouch position and helped them unhook from the line.

Stu shivered uncontrollably. Mike was beyond that stage. His muscles were no longer shivering and he was nearly incoherent. Stu said that he was afraid to let the fixed line drop for fear that it may get hung up, thereby trapping us on the ledge. We put Mike and Stu in the center of our group scrum, hoping to get some measure of warmth back into their bodies. Within minutes of their return to the Notch, the rain turned to a pasty, wet sleet. Clouds boiled down the cliff, and only the lower half of our 300-foot fixed line was now visible.

Kyle left the scrum and headed for the fixed line. Out of the lee of the Spire, he was exposed to more sleet and the continual spray from the falls. He quickly attached his ascenders and headed up. Kelly announced that he was going next.

We decided that only two would be on the line at a time. I knew this would be problematic, as we could not see the rim to be able to tell when the line was free. Before Kelly left the scrum, I told him to give out a loud shout when he could see that Kyle had made the top. Everyone understood that this would be the process.

Kelly left the scrum once Kyle was about eighty feet up the rope. The wall was now running with a steady stream of water.

Kyle was moving painfully slowly. In perfect conditions, the ascent of this much rope would normally take about ten minutes. Kyle had been on the rope that long and wasn't even at the halfway point yet. In a few minutes, Kelly had reached his brother. They were both being blasted by sheets of spray that swept across the wall. Within minutes, Kelly was rappelling back down. Not a good sign. Once he reached the ledge, Kyle started rappelling as well.

Kelly joined us back in the scrum. With teeth chattering, he told us that Kyle was in real bad shape and simply could not tolerate the effort required to ascend the rope due to the worsening conditions. The higher he went on the line, the more severe the drenching. A few minutes later, Kyle joined us. He was in tears. His body trembled with mass convulsions. We rubbed his arms and legs as fast as possible, and both he and his brother seemed to recover a bit of warmth. Huddled here in the lee of the Spire, conditions were barely tolerable, and we talked out our options.

We thought perhaps one of us could make it up the line and go for help. Carl was in the best physical shape and was coping with the cold better than the rest of us. However, he had never used ascenders before, and we were all concerned with how he would manage at the halfway point where he would have to carefully pass the knot in the line. This requires taking one ascender off the line at a time and reattaching it above the knot, then repeat the process with the second ascender. Though a simple move, it had the potential for mistakes for someone suffering from numb hands and slowing brain function.

Even if Carl did make it out, I was equally concerned with the thought of us huddling on the ledge all day waiting for help to arrive. I knew all too well that warding off hypothermia took physical action, not sitting idle. The benefits of the scrum would last only so long. It was now about 11:00 a.m., and any rescue would likely come well after dark.

Mike suggested that Tonya and Michelle, his and Stu's

girlfriends, were probably watching our progress and would have alerted the Park Service of our predicament. He felt that rescue was most likely on the way, and we should just stay and wait it out. I chimed in that the girls could also be just lounging around the Village shops, completely oblivious to our situation, which elicited a foul-mouthed rebuke from Mike.

While a teeth-chattering debate raged on the subject of rescue, I thought about the possibility of rappelling to the base of the wall from the Notch. We had the benefit of four ropes at our disposal, since Mike and Stu had elected to use the double rope technique. Each rope was 165 feet long. I estimated that we were about 1,200 feet above the base of the wall. With two ropes tied together, we could manage 160-foot rappels and then set up the next rappel with the second set of ropes. Once everyone was down the initial rappel, the rope would be pulled down through the anchor, and set up below the second rappel line, and so on. Of course, this assumed we would find cracks that would provide anchor placements to support our system. I was unsure if the wall had any established routes that could provide pre-placed anchors. As I looked down the wall, it appeared to me that it might be doable with the gear we had.

Back in the scrum, I suggested the idea of rappelling the wall. Stu and Mike were against it straight away. They were convinced the girls were alerting the authorities and felt we should wait. Everyone was concerned that we might get down the wall for a certain distance, only to run out of anchor placement opportunities. Once we pulled the ropes above us, we would be committed to rappelling the wall, or having to climb back up, if that were possible. I wasn't arguing their point; certainly the risks were huge.

With all of us entering severely hypothermic states, the chances were great that we could do something out of sheer, cold-induced stupidity. I just felt that movement was better than not moving at all, and that if we stayed, we may die of hypothermia right on that ledge. Again, I reminded everyone that we had no way of knowing whether the girls had alerted the park service. We could try to wait out the weather, but at what cost?

Clouds cascaded down onto our position and continued down the wall towards the valley. The wet sleet had mostly quit, but we were enveloped in a constant, heat-draining mist. The wind continued to blow the spray from the falls right through the Notch. All of us had passed the point of shivering; I knew our bodies were starting to shut down. It was about then that I got mad.

I gathered the gear we had for anchors, and started to tie two of our ropes together. Carl, Kelly and Kyle were all for my idea. The fear that showed on their faces had turned to resolve to do something. Anything was better than sitting there getting colder by the minute. Stu began to give in, but Mike had a stubborn will. I went up to him, stuck my face right in his, and as loud as I could, screamed, "If we stay here, we die here!"

I fixed the rope to the anchor on the ledge and explained my plan. I would rappel to the end of one set of ropes and see if I could find a spot to set another anchor. Then I would survey the wall to see if it looked feasible for us to continue down. If I reached a dead end, I would ascend back up the ropes. If I thought we could continue, I would tell Carl to come down after me and bring the other two ropes with him, and I would begin setting up the next rappel.

For safety, I tied the ends of the rappel lines together to keep myself from rappelling off the end of the line. I tossed the ropes off the ledge and watched as they disappeared into the clouds. Clipped into the line, I looked everyone in the eye.

"Wish me luck."

I stepped back off the ledge and started down. Though I tried not to let it show back in the scrum, I was terrified. My only consolation was that I was moving. Up to this point, I had been praying silently. Now alone and hanging in the mist on that sheer wall, I prayed out loud.

"Lord, show me the way. Lord, show me the way."

About a hundred feet down I came out of the clouds, which was a relief. It had quit sleeting, and I now realized that I was no longer being affected by the spray of the falls in this position. There was a bit more wind, but my skin was drying off. I was still terribly cold. The clouds had extended across the valley, blocking any sunshine. My shorts and t-shirt had been soaked through for hours, and when I had the urge, I simply urinated in my shorts.

I was rappelling down a large crack system located in a corner created by the wall on one side, and the bulk of the spire on the other. About twenty feet shy of the knot at the end of my ropes, I found a spot for a solid anchor. Normally, a minimum of three pieces of hardware would constitute an acceptable anchor. I thought perhaps I should try and conserve and keep it to two pieces, but with as many as four guys on the equipment at a time, I erred on the side of making the anchors as bombproof as I could.

As I tried to set the anchor pieces in the crack, I realized that my hands were not functioning well. My fingers had been numb for hours, and now trying to handle more nimble tasks was an effort. I was careful not to drop anything, as it looked as if we would use up our entire collection of gear to get down the wall. Unfortunately, this first anchor consumed our three largest pieces of protection.

With the anchor complete, I clipped myself in and surveyed the situation. The large crack I was in continued down for at least another rope length. If it stayed wide like this present location, I would not have the gear for an anchor. I could see potential anchor locations in a corner system off to my right, but we would have to do some wild traversing. A few hundred feet down that corner was a small tree growing from what appeared to be a narrow ledge. From that spot, it looked as if the crack system continued all the way to the base.

I called up to the Notch, or at least tried to. My jaws had been clenched from the cold and the fear, and I was having difficulty getting out a loud yell. I rubbed on my face with my hands, cupping them over my mouth and blowing out warm air. Within a few minutes I was functioning a little better.

I called out, "I think it will go!"

Carl heard my call, and a moment later, yelled out that he was heading down.

My muscles had become painfully stiff, and I tried to move around as much as I could. I swung my arms in a windmill motion and stomped my feet against the wall. I pulled off the small pack I was wearing and tried to eat some food and swallow some water. Though I was hungry, my stomach was having a hard time dealing with anything. Hours of relentless fear had made me quite sick, but I knew that my metabolism would benefit from any fuel I could get down. I managed to swallow a bagel and some dried fruit.

The cold was unbearable, but I had long since resigned myself to it. What I would have given for a knit hat though. Most body heat is lost from the head and neck. I beat myself up pretty good for not bringing additional clothing.

Carl appeared out of the clouds and minutes later, arrived with the other two ropes over his shoulders. He quickly clipped in next to me at the anchor. He yelled up and let the guys know the rope was free for the next man. I asked him how things were back up on the ledge.

"A lot wetter than here," he replied.

"How are the other guys doing?"

"Mike and Stu are going downhill fast."

The plan was for them to rappel next. He said that both of them were experiencing the same difficulties that I was having with not being able to speak very well. I asked Carl how he was feeling.

"Probably better than you look! Your lips are blue and your face is stark white."

I knew he was seriously cold too, but he was doing a great job of staying in the game.

Carl and I set about tying the two ropes together and looped them through the new anchor point. Kyle yelled down that Stu and Mike were on the ropes and heading our way.

I asked Carl if he would pray with me, and together we asked God for protection. We prayed for the other guys, mainly that none of us would make any mistakes.

With the ropes securely looped through the anchor, we dropped the lines down the wall and I clipped in. As I started my rappel, I told Carl to try to get everyone to eat something.

"And tell the guys not to pull the ropes from above until I give a sign from below that I think we can continue down this way."

He wished me luck, and I slid down the lines.

As I began to descend, I looked up and saw Mike and Stu come into view. Once again they were simul-rappelling, rappelling together down a rope that is looped through an anchor with the ends together below them, as they had from off the Spire, which was probably a good idea. Together, they could monitor each other's progress and encourage one another. It would also speed up the process and get Kyle and Kelly moving sooner.

I continued down the corner crack system with the hopes of seeing it taper into something smaller and more acceptable of our gear. Looking down towards the ends of the ropes, I realized that in our haste, Carl and I had forgotten to tie the two ends together. As I approached the ends, I would have to be extremely careful and keep a firm grip on the lines. The good news was that the wind was lessened at this level, and I noticed that my shirt was drying a bit.

With about thirty feet of rope left, I saw the crack coming to an end, and my heart sank. It was still too big for the gear I had remaining on the rack slung over my shoulder. The bile rose in my throat, and a feeling of dread crept in. Up above, Stu and Mike were safely with Carl, and the brothers were on their way.

"This spot isn't gonna' work!" I yelled up to Carl. "I'm gonna' have to look for something else!"

Then I saw it. Near the bottom of the crack was a good-sized chockstone, a rock wedged tightly in the crack that offered a natural anchor. I lowered myself until I was chest level with the chock. I tied myself off with the rappel line. Pulling on the rock, I was elated to find it solid.

"I've found a spot!" I yelled up to Carl.

He let out a loud, "Whoop!"

With two slings tied together, I managed to tie a girth hitch around the chockstone. I felt totally confident in it as our next anchor. I had the sudden urge to pee and simply let it go again in my shorts.

Looking down from this spot there was only one clear option: a small traverse right to the left-facing corner system I had spotted from above. It looked as if we might even make it to that small tree on the next rappel. I yelled up to Carl and pointed out my observation. Above him I could see Kyle and Kelly simul-rappelling like Stu and Mike had. They were moving slowly, but making steady progress.

We were now at nearly the point of no return. To continue we would have to pull the first set of ropes from the Notch. Carl came down and joined me at the rock anchor. He complimented my ingenuity and thought it looked good, and then asked how I was doing.

"I'm cold but okay," I replied.

I pointed to the tree and my intended line of travel heading down from the tree ledge. With chattering teeth, Carl voiced his approval, and at the same time used some choice words to describe the daunting exposure. The wall below us was nearly vertical all the way to the base.

The brothers had reached the anchor above.

"We're heading down and right!" Carl yelled up.

With that news, Kelly lowered the rope to us, as Kyle pulled the line from the Notch. Once the end of the rope reached us, Carl and I threaded it through the anchor and let it drop. We kept the end tied off, so that we could tie it to the other end once it dropped down.

With the system set, I clipped in and began my descending traverse to the right. Stu and Mike headed down to Carl. As I

moved out away from Carl and the relative protection of the
corner system, I felt the wind again. It caused more shivers to run
through me, which I took as a good sign, since I thought I was past
the shivering stage of hypothermia.

I had to push hard with my left leg to keep moving to my right
across the wall. I saw that the knot at the end of the ropes was
near the level of the tree. Above, Stu and Mike had made it down
to Carl. The brothers waited until I had the next anchor in place,
as there was little room at the chockstone anchor.

Straining against the pendulum affect, I pushed my way closer
to the corner system, and with about six feet of rope to spare, I
made it to the small ledge with the tree. The base of the pine was
about five inches in diameter. It proved to be a superb anchor and,
once again, we were going to be able to save some much-needed
gear. I was thrilled with both the tree and the benefit of actually
having a small place to stand. This tiny ledge was an island of
horizontal in a sea of vertical, and it helped calm my frayed
nerves. Tied off and the line secured, I called for Carl to come on
down.

Though the ledge gave us a small place to stand, we were now
exposed to the brunt of the wind gusts. However, I did notice that
my shirt and shorts were now nearly dry. Once again, I pulled off
my pack, drank some water, and gobbled a little food. I knew I had
to keep my metabolism fed, but my stomach was in knots. I had to
work at swallowing anything at all.

Carl had given way and let Stu and Mike on the line, and
shortly they were at the ledge. With the brothers now down to the
chockstone anchor, Carl coiled the ropes from above around his
shoulders while the brothers pulled. In a few minutes Carl was on
his way to the ledge.

Mike and Stu hunkered on the ledge with their backs to the
wind. Neither of them was interested in food, but I talked them
into a piece of beef jerky anyway. Their lack of conversation told
me they were really hurting from the cold. It was clear that the
time they had spent getting soaked on the Spire had sapped much

of their strength.

Carl arrived at the ledge cursing and swearing the coils of wet rope that he had piled around his shoulders and neck. I reminded him that at least it wasn't sleeting anymore. And the wet rope stretched a little more than normal, allowing us to get a bit further on each rappel.

We looped the ropes around the tree, tied the ends together, and cast them down the wall. As I clipped in to the lines, I whispered to Carl, "Try and get Stu and Mike to eat more."

He agreed, and I started down the lines once again, as the brothers descended to the ledge.

The crack system continued angling down the wall to the right. Once again I was working hard with my left leg in order to keep pushing myself towards the crack. The cracks were narrower here, and small enough to accept the gear I had. From my vantage point I could not tell if the crack stayed on the smaller side, but I had been going on faith up to this point. So far so good.

I was nearing the end of the ropes when suddenly, over the sound of the falls and the wind, I heard a bullhorn blast coming from the west, in the direction of the falls trail.

"On the wall! Wave if you can hear me!"

Looking in the direction of the voice, I made out a small group on the trail. Initially dumbfounded, I waved like a madman.

"Wave again if your party is all together!"

I waved my arms again.

"Wave again if you need assistance!"

As I waved, I heard screams from above and looked up to see all five guys waving like crazed lunatics.

The voice on the bullhorn went quiet, but above me the hollering continued. Carl was clapping his hands like a man possessed, and the brothers were whooping it up with all kinds of shouts and whistles. Stu and Mike huddled at the tree, lying against the wall in the classic spoon position, but at least they were showing some signs of life. Clearly, they were in far worse shape than the rest of us. I quietly prayed that they could make it on their own without us having to lower them.

With adrenaline back in my veins, I swung across the wall to the right in hopes of finding another suitable anchor position. I tried to get into a bit of a run across the wall, but my legs were not working well. It was all I could do just to push myself slowly in a diagonal traverse.

Every minute or so Carl yelled down, "Anything?" I kept shaking my head no.

I pushed myself tightly into the corner with all my strength. With about twenty feet of rope left, my effort was rewarded; I had found our next anchor spot. There was even a small stance area for my feet with enough room for another to stand alongside me. I tried to yell up to the guys, but nothing came out of my mouth. My throat felt like I had swallowed a pound of sand with a cotton ball chaser.

Carl yelled down, "Did you find something?" I signaled him with a thumbs-up.

The crack was small and slightly horizontal, but it would take solid small- to medium-stopper placements. I fumbled to get the aluminum wedge with its swage of cable into the crack just right. My hands struggled to attach the rope to the cable loop with a carabiner. What would normally have been about five minutes of effort, took me nearly twenty. I completed the anchor and clipped myself in solid.

Again, I tried to yell to Carl, but I could not manage anything audible over the wind. My teeth were now clenched, and I realized I was getting much colder. I waved to Carl and he started down towards me, bringing the ropes.

I wasn't sure what time it was, but, based on the angle of the light, I guessed about four in the afternoon. If that were the case, we had about four hours of daylight left. Carl moved toward me as I surveyed the wall below for our next move. The crack continued to angle down and right. This angle worked to our advantage, as the ground rose up to meet the wall much faster the farther to the right the crack went. It also looked as if the crack were going to stay on the small side. Carl arrived, clipped in next to me, and we threaded the ropes through the anchor.

"You ok?" he asked.

Through clenched teeth I managed a meager, "I'm dealing with it."

We hugged each other and rubbed each other's back furiously.

"How are things up there?" I muttered, as I nodded towards the group above.

"We all got pretty excited when we heard the bullhorn. Mike said, 'I told you the girls would report us in trouble and that we should have stayed put.'"

I just shook my head as Carl continued.

"The brothers are doing okay, but Mike and Stu are in bad shape."

"Have they had anything to eat?" I whispered.

"Kyle and Kelly were eating some candy, and I did too, but Stu and Mike are just too out of it."

I looked at Carl.

"What about you?"

"I'm alright," he responded in a soft voice.

I knew he was lying. His lips were now as blue as he had said mine were earlier, and he looked weary. At the same time, I saw resolve in his eyes. I knew we were all treading water, just trying to hold on as long as possible.

Back toward the trail, the small group of rescuers was nowhere to be seen. We weren't sure what their plans were, but we knew we needed to keep going.

I connected my rappel device to the ropes. Carl mentioned that Mike had defecated in his shorts.

"Well, I've pissed mine numerous times over the course of the day," I said, "so I won't hold it against him."

Flashing Carl a faint smile, I started down, and it occurred to me that Mike's body may be shutting down dramatically.

As I headed down, it appeared we had about 500 feet to go. My legs felt especially heavy after hanging at the anchor for the past thirty minutes. In fact, my whole body was tight. I felt incredibly clumsy as I moved. I pushed with my legs as hard as they would work to keep making my way to the right.

As I descended, the crack widened, and I grew concerned. I had only one piece left that would possibly work well in a larger crack: a medium-sized retractable, spring-loaded cam. As I neared the knot at the end of the lines, the crack narrowed a bit, and I went to work on an anchor.

As I pulled the trigger bar back on the cam, it narrowed into the crack. I released the trigger bar and the cam locked itself in place. Then I clipped myself to it so that I could relax a bit as I worked on the rest of the anchor. The cam was absolutely bombproof, but we couldn't risk utilizing a one-piece anchor for so much weight.

My heart raced with the thought of being stranded after having come so far. I reached to the back of my harness for one of the two locking carabiners I had with me, thinking I might be able to use it as a stopper placement. As I brought the carabiner from behind me, I bumped it against the rack of gear hanging from my shoulder and watched in horror as it rocketed down the wall.

"Damn it!" I cursed, as I watched the piece ricochet down the rock. I was on the verge of either crying or getting hysterical.

My mind raced. I lost track of time. I reached back again for my one remaining locking carabiner. After what seemed like hours of frustrating fumbling, I managed to get the carabiner wedged in a reasonably tight position just above the cam. I tied three slings together and clipped them into the carabiner, then stuck one foot through the slings and stepped as hard as I could. The carabiner ground into the crack and held firm. I shortened the sling, combined the tied off carabiner with the cam, and declared the anchor complete; it was all I was going to get. I tied the rappel line in to the anchor and waved up to Carl.

As I looked up, I was amazed to see that Carl now had Mike, Stu and Kyle with him at the anchor, and Kelly was rappelling down to them. I couldn't believe they had moved that fast.

As Carl rappelled to me, I was startled once again by the voice on the bullhorn.

"You guys are doing great!"

It had been a good two hours since our last contact with them. In fact, I had almost completely forgotten about them. But there they were, hiking up to the base of the wall. They were nearly directly below us. I was elated by the mere sight of them. Tears rolled down my face. They moved effortlessly as they traversed the slope below. I wanted to be on the ground with them in the worst way. I tried to call out to them, but nothing got through my severely clenched teeth. I knew I was losing it.

Carl arrived. I could see concern on his face as he clipped himself in.

"Are you alright?"

Pointing down the wall, I chattered, "Look. They're right there."

"Yeah. I see that. But what happened to your hands?"

I looked down at my hands, which were a bloody mess. The anchor was covered in blood. I could only figure that I had bashed my hands trying to set the carabiner. I told Carl I didn't remember hurting myself. He surveyed my quasi-carabiner anchor.

"What do you call that?"

"A little bit of ingenuity and a lot of desperation."

Quietly Carl mumbled, "We gotta' get the hell off this wall."

As Kyle moved down the rope from above, Carl and I did some more hugging. Without warning, he slapped my face hard.

"Just checking."

I slapped him right back.

"Me too."

We both managed a little grin. I ate some candy and drank a bit of water, then promptly peed in my shorts again.

The crack system we were in continued down for another thirty feet or so, and another fifty feet of rope hung below our present anchor. I clipped myself onto the line and readied to rappel again.

"Are you still up for this?" Carl asked. I nodded a simple "yes" and kept going.

I reached the knot at the end of the ropes and clipped my ascenders into the rappel lines, so I could relax a bit. Mike and Stu were rappelling down to Carl. We were getting close to the end, in more ways than one. I knew I was losing control. Something about seeing those eight guys at the base of the wall stirring around and readying for our arrival made me want to give up. I just didn't want to deal with it anymore.

I thought about trying to reach the ground with the last two ropes tied end to end in one continuous rappel. We'd get about 340 feet with the stretch in the ropes. As if they were reading my mind, the guy on the bullhorn yelled up.

"It looks like you have two rope lengths to go!" That was all the confirmation I needed. I tried to yell back, but could only manage a weak wave.

Carl was able to yell down to them and explain our condition.

"If you don't think you can manage, we can climb up to you!" they yelled back.

"Wha'd'ya' think?" Carl asked.

"I can work out an anchor right here," I said. "You have Mike and Stu stay on the rappel line. Don't let them clip into that funky anchor until I get this one complete, and you're down here with me."

I fumbled with a menagerie of stoppers and promptly dropped one. I began to sob. With tears welling in my eyes, I mumbled out a prayer as I battled with my stiff fingers. After about forty-five minutes, I managed to link two pair of stoppers into a solid anchor backed up with a single stopper that was marginal at best. I called Carl down, and Mike and Stu moved onto the anchor as Carl left. The brothers, who had been waiting patiently, began to rappel from above.

In short order, Carl was once again by my side.

"Can I have some of your water," I said. "Mine's all gone."

"Yah. Mine's all gone, too. Sorry."

I sighed. Time to move on.

"Have Mike or Stu come down to this anchor to leave room for Kelly and Kyle above," I said in a voice barely audible. "I don't like the idea of having even three on that funky anchor."

I hung limp at the anchor and felt only half conscious. Mike came down to us exuding an odor and foulness that defied explanation. I thought *I* was a sorry sight. His shorts and harness were caked with feces. Carl explained to him what we were going to do. I chimed in that he would have to clip his ascenders to the rope at the halfway point in order to release his rappel device to get past the knot. He nodded and said he could do it.

With Kelly and Kyle clipped in above with Stu, the brothers pulled the rope from above and lowered it to us. We tied a knot in the low end and let it snake down the wall, carefully holding it tight as the other end drew near. Carl tied a knot in the end and I clipped it into the anchor.

The bullhorn shrieked, "That'll work! We can help you from there!"

The line was a good fifty feet short, but had reached some lower angled terrain. Carl and I decided to put Mike on the rope first in case he needed help with passing the knot. With Mike clipped in, we sent him on his way. He flashed us a weak smile, but his eyes looked like he was miles away. He was a fraction of the man who had charged up the trail early that morning. I knew I wasn't looking much better.

The team on the ground had been busy. Two plastic tarps had been erected as tents, and a team was climbing to the base of our line with a line of their own. For the first time since we began our descent, I allowed my mind to believe that this odyssey was actually almost over.

Carl and I breathed a sigh of relief as Mike negotiated the passing of the knot without incident. He moved slow but steady. In a matter of minutes he was in the arms of a rescuer. Tears streamed down Carl's and my faces, as the brothers let out whoops from above. With amazing speed, the rescuers had Mike all the way to the ground and moved into one of the tents.

Stu came down and clipped into the single line straight away. The sight of Mike getting down had given him a shot of adrenaline, so we told him to just keep moving. Very quickly he made the transition at the knot and moved on down the line.

Carl and I looked at each other. He gave me a hug, followed by another good slap in the face.

"Get outta here!" he said. I smiled, clipped into the line, and headed down.

I remember very little after passing the knot. I was told later that when I reached the arms of the rescuers I was mumbling incoherently, I could not undo my rappel device, and urine was running down my legs. They carried me to the tent.

The next thing I knew, I was sitting in a sleeping bag, buck-naked. My body was racked with pain. I was under some sort of makeshift tent with open ends, and I could see it was dark out. I was leaned against a bunch of large packs as somebody fed me a cup of warm bullion soup, while they rattled off one question after another. Mike and Stu were in the tent as well, getting the same treatment.

I was told everyone was down safely, that we were being warmed and fed, and then we would be hiking down to the village when we were ready. I was in no hurry. As far as I was concerned, that little tent was the Ahwanhee Lodge. It was nearly 9:00 p.m.

A few hours later, dressed in a hodgepodge of foul weather gear, we began a long, grueling hike through a tangle of bushes and steep rock bands and gullies. I was practically out on my feet, but I was warm, and that's all that mattered to me at that moment. Once down in the valley, we were driven over to the clinic for a check-up.

Though we were all bleary-eyed, bruised and battered, we were otherwise all right. The doctor wanted to put us on I.V. fluids, but we all refused in favor of the food and warm drink being supplied to us by Michelle and Tonya and a few nurses.

We spent the next few hours telling our story to a Park Service employee, so that he could fill out his report. It turned out the girls had been watching us from Yosemite Village and had indeed, reported us as "potentially in trouble." The girls had insisted that we had not taken adequate clothing for the freak conditions, which caused the Park Service to respond.

The rescuers said they had spotted us when I was making the arcing traverse over to the corner crack system. That trail team radioed the valley for assistance and directed another team to hike up to the base to meet us. The trail team then continued to the top in case a rescue were needed from above. They were even kind enough to retrieve our rappel lines hanging from the rim, which they said had been caked in slush near the top.

At dawn, with copious amounts of thanks, we said our good-byes to the clinic staff and made our way back to Camp 4. We sat around a picnic table and basked in the warm, morning sun. Collectively, we had lost a lot of our gear, but we had no regrets about it. Even Mike conceded that it worked out for the better to have kept moving. The clouds and wind had not abated until after midnight.

They all decided to pack up and make their way home. By noon their van was loaded and ready to go. I was still reeling from all that had transpired and found it hard to say good-bye. It was most difficult with Carl.

Clearly, he was the most inexperienced member of our little group. Yet he was always by my side offering encouragement. I gave him a hug.

"Thanks for staying with me."

He looked me in the eye and said, 'Thanks for praying with me."

I handed them a piece of paper with my address and phone number and told them to keep in touch. Below the address I wrote, "Let's go climbing next time!"

Once they had gone, I wandered over to Curry Village and took an impossibly long, hot shower. Afterward, I hopped on the shuttle bus to make my way back to the campground. I got off the bus in Yosemite Village, bought myself an ice cream cone, and took a seat on a bench that commanded a fine view of the Lost Arrow.

I followed the line of our descent route and could clearly see the small tree we had rappelled from. As I thought back through the emotions of the previous day, the memories made me shiver. With a fervent prayer, I thanked God for the guidance and protection he had provided us. I couldn't help but think that one of his guardian angels had been living inside of Carl.

I wondered if I would ever get to do that famous Tyrolean Traverse. I was certain of one thing: if I did get the chance to climb the Spire again, I'd check the weather forecast and go prepared for anything.

I crawled into my tent that night and fell into a deep sleep. The next morning I packed my belongings, loaded my truck, and headed out of the valley. Later that day, as I arrived home, a friend stopped by and asked how my trip had been. I thought about it briefly then replied, "Memorable."

Over the course of the summer I often thought about those five guys and the extraordinary day we shared on the Lost Arrow Spire. In hindsight, I realized that I had learned valuable lessons from each of them. I remembered my initial impression of Stu and Mike as we hiked up the falls trail that morning thinking they would be the leaders that day, with the rest of us in tow. As the day's events played out, their collective experience and leadership were humbled by the effects of the weather, rendering them almost a liability rather than an asset. I would come to respect the weather and its ability to control even the most qualified of leaders.

The lasting impression I had of Kelly and Kyle was one of teamwork and perseverance. The visual of the pair of them attempting to ascend the fixed line in the teeth of the stinging rain is a reminder that we always have to give any effort our best shot. Their quiet patience while waiting their turn on the rappels, realizing that the difficulty and seriousness of the situation required hunkering down and just dealing with the cold, was testament to their character. And their almost maniacal exuberance when we first heard the bullhorn I will never forget.

I believe it was Carl, though, from whom I learned the most that day. Though a young man of great physical strength, he was clearly the least experienced member of our party. However, he was willing to put all trust in the rest of us to make good decisions, and his quiet faith in our abilities made us all stronger.

Carl had proved to be my barometer. He gave me pats on the back and encouragement when I did well and much-needed slaps in the face when my own spirit was waning. To this day, I believe it was Carl's quiet strength and personal companionship that got us all down. I learned then never to underestimate the value of any team member.

The summer gave way to fall, the high country grew too cold for climbing, and I spent my climbing days on the warm, high desert crags in Joshua Tree. Sitting by my campfire one evening enjoying the stars, I saw a figure approaching in the darkness, and for a moment I thought it was Carl. As the man entered the firelight I realized it was Earl, a climber and recent acquaintance. Sitting around the fire that evening, we laid out plans for climbing together the next morning.

I doused the fire for the evening, bid Earl goodnight, and climbed into my tent. Pulling off my shirt, I noticed the bloodstains on it. It was the shirt I'd been wearing that day on the Spire. It was a stark reminder of an event that would shape the rest of my years, and I secretly hoped that those five young men had learned as much as I did.

I never heard from them again.

CHAPTER 4

. . . for death is the destiny of every man;
the living should take this to heart.

Ecclesiastes 7:2

In October of 1984, a three-and-a-half-year-old girl named Laura Bradbury, disappeared from her family campsite in Joshua Tree National Park. This event tugged at my heart like nothing before. I had been climbing in Joshua Tree for years, knew it well, and had grown to love the place. The thought of what a young family was going through with their daughter missing drew me in to the world of search and rescue, or SAR.

The search continued for the next two and a half years, when skeletal remains were finally found. Over that course of time, I spent 162 days searching. Though I personally never found a single thing that was linked to Laura, being able to use my years of climbing and backcountry skills in the effort to help others just felt right. Volunteering as a SAR professional became my passion.

In May of 1989, my new wife, Leah, and I moved to the eastern high Sierra. I had a work opportunity in the ski town of Mammoth Lakes. I had been climbing in the Sierra since the '70s, but living there seemed a distant dream. Now, I was living that dream, in arguably the best spot on the planet for a rock climber. Yosemite was just minutes away, and the entire heart of the range was at my doorstep. It didn't take long to find climbing partners, as well as the opportunity to work on one of the busiest SAR teams in the nation.

Within weeks of arriving in Mammoth Lakes, I began climbing with Doug Nidever, a long-time climber and guide and a member of the Mono County Sheriff Search and Rescue Team. It was Doug who introduced me to the world of ice climbing, and I was soon hooked on climbing the frozen waterfalls throughout the region. It was through my friendship with Doug that I met Pete Schoerner.

I'd describe Pete as a complete man's man. He works as a paramedic for the county, as well as a ski patrolman and SAR team volunteer. Pete is the guy you can count on, and the list of lives he has saved over the years is legendary.

He is also an extreme guy in everything he does. From skiing, to rock and ice climbing, kayaking, and mountain bike racing, Pete goes full tilt, a pedal-to-the-metal kind of guy. And when it comes to SAR missions, Pete is the first one out the door. He is also a devoted father of three and loves his kids intensely. To say I respect this man is a gross understatement.

I've always admired people who are so dedicated to SAR that they drop whatever they're doing and go at a moment's notice. In 1986, a spotter was needed to go up in a search plane to look for a pair of missing hikers. Along with fellow team member Rick Mosher, Pete volunteered. With only one seat available, a coin was flipped, and Rick won. During the search, the plane clipped a wing on a cliff side, and both the pilot and Rick were killed. In spite of this near-death experience, Pete never wavers in his dedication. To him, the risk is simply part of the deal.

Because of his deep skill and experience, Pete is usually the first SAR member the sheriff calls when the team is needed. Back then, we lived in a world that was pre-cell phone or pager technology, so we used the land-line-phone-tree system. Once Pete discovered my passion and experience with SAR, my phone rang with every event. Pete and I logged plenty of miles together, climbing, skiing, and responding to SAR calls.

In the fall of 1995, a solo hiker took a fatal 800-foot fall down an ice-choked chute on one of our local peaks. Along with fellow team member Joe Rousek, Pete, Doug and I hiked in to do the recovery. We found the body lodged in a narrow crevasse. Being the smallest of the four of us, Pete got the duty of going down into the crevasse to secure a line to the body, then pushing from below. What Pete lacked in stature, he made up for in a whatever-it-takes attitude. Together, we recovered the body, which was flown out of the backcountry in a chopper.

Days later, a tourist drowned while wading in Hot Creek, a local stream heated by geothermal water. The body had washed downstream and into a particularly hot pool of boiling water, where it became trapped. As the water bubbled up dramatically from below, we caught sight of the body coming up then watched it disappear once again in the churning cauldron.

Pete dressed in a neoprene dry suit normally used for lake ice rescue, and we put him in a small raft and pulled him out into the middle of the creek. He snagged the victim with a large grappling hook. Just days before we had been dealing with a frozen corpse; now, we were extricating a body that had been boiled like a chicken. The body was literally coming apart.

To date, this is the most gruesome thing I have ever witnessed. Pete never flinched. He just did the job. We bagged the body, or what was left of it, and I went home shaken by the vision. Pete never thought about it again. The job was done.

"Just move on and be ready for the next one," is his mantra.

It wouldn't be long before I saw the value in his thinking and adopted it for myself. It was simply self-preservation. Do the job, but don't dwell on it.

Pete, Doug and I all lived within a few minutes of each other in June Lake, and, as New Year of 1996 rolled around, the three of us noticed a new ice flow forming on a local cliff. With ideal, cold conditions, it continued to grow to the point where it looked as if, very soon, it would be climbable.

The flow developed in the form of what we call a fang, or pillar. These formations are created by water dripping over an overhanging section of rock, creating a pillar attached at the top and bottom of the ice, but detached from the rest of the rock wall.

It appeared to be about forty feet tall, but was located in the middle of a 700 foot-high cliff face. As the days went by, we watched in anticipation as it grew.

In mid-January, Doug's wife called me one morning and said that Doug was overdue from guiding a client on Carson Peak, the mountain right out our front door. Conditions were desperately cold and snowy, and the SAR team was called out. Pete and I, along with fellow SAR team member John Ellsworth, were given the task of ascending the peak by different routes in an attempt to locate the pair. Our minds reeled with the thought of possibly having to recover the body of our friend, but we steeled ourselves for the task with hopes of a positive outcome.

A few hours later, I came across the two of them, alive and well and descending the peak in deep snow. They had been delayed by the conditions and the client's lack of good conditioning for the effort required. The events of the previous few months had shown us enough death, and it was a relief to find them alive and well. With Doug safely back, we turned our attention to that fang of ice.

Over the next few days we hatched our plan. The ice was looking strong enough to warrant an attempt for this coveted first ascent. Scanning the route with binoculars, we could see it would require climbing 400 feet up a steep rock wall coated with delicate, thin ice sections, just to reach the pillar. From the top of the pillar, another 250 feet of tricky rock climbing led to the summit.

Reviewing our combined work schedules, we decided on a day for the attempt on the fang. Then the weather changed. An approaching storm system was pushing warmer air in front of it, and it appeared that the ice would not last much longer. Two nights before our intended climb, Pete called.

"We need to get on it tomorrow, or we're gonna' lose the chance!"

Doug was keen, but I had an inspection scheduled on one of my construction projects that I simply could not miss. I was out.

Dejected, I wished them good luck, and told them I would keep an eye on them from my job site, which commanded a fine view of the entire wall.

January 29, 1996
June Lake, California

The wind had blown hard all night. The approaching weather system was getting closer. With the wind came warmer temperatures, and at dawn it was thirty-three degrees. Through intermittent cloud cover, the wall was occasionally bathed in bright sunshine, good for the body, but not for the ice. From my vantage, I watched as Doug and Pete made their way up the steep snowfield below the wall to its base.

With my inspection out of the way early, I turned my sole focus to their progress. With binoculars, I was practically close enough to see their breath clouds. I watched, mesmerized, as they weaved their way up the wall for hours to the base of the fang.

With a belay set in the rock wall just below and left of the base of the pillar, Pete took over the lead. He swung his axes and kicked in the metal spikes of the crampons on his climbing boots, as he ascended lower-angled ice to gain the base of the fang.

A nice ledge had formed in the ice at the pillar's base, giving Pete ample time to rest before beginning to climb the dead vertical column. With Pete now standing next to the fang, I could more adequately gauge its size. It was at its narrowest at the base, about five feet in diameter. As it rose, it increased to about eight feet thick and appeared to be about forty-five feet tall.

One safely ascends a normal ice flow by inserting an ice screw into the ice as an anchor. The screws come in different lengths depending on the thickness of the ice. A standard screw is about eight inches long and three-quarters of an inch in diameter. The screws have an eyelet to which the rope is clipped. Should the climber fall, the screw performs the same job a piece of rock protection would provide; it arrests a fall.

Though fairly massive in size, this fang formation was still delicate and suspect. The standard procedure for climbing a fang is to initially climb up the rock behind the column, and set anchors in the rock wall. Then come back to the base and ascend the ice. In this way, should the ice collapse while climbing on it, the climber can swing back to the wall, out of the way of the falling ice, with solid anchors catching the fall. An ice screw into the formation would only bring disaster should the ice depart the wall, dragging the climber down with it.

At some point, Pete disappeared behind the column to set his anchors. Doug was hanging from his harness at the belay that had been set in the rock to secure his climbing rope about thirty feet below. While Pete was out of view, I grabbed a chair and made myself comfortable. Though I was disappointed I wasn't there with them, I had a perfect view of the climb and sat back to enjoy the show. I had a two-way radio with me that I used to keep in touch with other job sites and with Leah back at the house. I called her and gave her an update on the guys' progress.

I had to admit I was envious of Doug. Hanging with Pete is always pure joy. He just has a way of making things special. Perhaps it's the way he sees stuff: with an adventurer's eye and a nice dose of madness. He always finds a way to make things more special than they already are.

Just days before, I had been on the ski area and had met up with Pete right at closing, as he was about to do his "sweep." Ski Patrolmen sweep once the ski area is closed, skiing along the edge of established runs, calling out into the trees to make sure no one is stuck or injured. When he invited me to join him I simply could not say "no."

It was one of those perfect eastern Sierra evenings. It had snowed most of the day then cleared in late afternoon. Two feet of fresh powder blanketed the mountain, and, as the sun set behind the crest, it set the sky on fire. Giant lenticular clouds shimmered like flying saucers high in the atmosphere, casting an orange glow down onto the snow. It was crisp and clear, and, with the ski area now closed, it was blissfully quiet.

"Hey Dean! You want to see something magical?"

"You bet, Pete." I began skating along behind him.

Almost immediately after leaving the lift tower at the very top of the mountain, Pete ducked under the boundary rope, and I followed. He poled his way through the knee-deep powder with me right behind. After a hundred yards or so, he stopped, and I glided up next to him.

I had been skiing on June Mountain for years, but had never seen anything so mesmerizing. The trees were adorned in a perfect cloak of fresh snow, their branches sagging from the weight. With the light of the sky refracting on the snow, the entire landscape took on an almost purple hue. In the distance, Mammoth Mountain and the entire Sherwin Range were lit by the setting sun. Further down the valley, the ice on Crowley Lake shimmered in a light blue cast, with the White Mountains beyond peeking out from low clouds. I'm not usually at a loss for words, but all I could say was, "Wow".

I looked over at Pete. He was taking it all in quietly, not saying a word. A few minutes went by, then softly, he said, "I usually don't bring people out here. This is a special spot for me. But I wanted you to see it."

"How come I'm the lucky one?" I quietly asked.

"You have a great heart, Dean. It would have been wrong for me not to share this with you."

I suddenly felt a lump in my throat. I have many spots that I call "my own," that I've never shared with others, and now Pete was letting me in to a place close to his own heart.

"Well, I sure appreciate it, Pete. I'll keep it to myself."

"Nah. Bring your kids up here when they get old enough. I've brought mine here, and that's why this spot is so special to me."

Pete flashed the huge, toothy smile that I had grown used to, especially when he was talking about his kids.

"Yeah. For sure I'll be bringing them out here, Pete. This is too good to pass up."

"Hey. It gets better. Follow me!"

Pete pulled his goggles down, and pushed off down the steepening slope. I followed just off his ski track in the fresh snow. I watched as Pete made perfect, graceful telemark turns out in front of me. Together we whooped and hollered our way down through the trees for hundreds of yards, as the powder washed up our legs and across our chests. In a few minutes, we turned back into the ski area boundary and came to a stop.

"Pretty amazing little shot there, eh?" Pete said, beaming his smile.

I practically shouted. "Dang, Pete! That was REALLY fine! Thanks for showing me that spot. I owe you one!"

We continued down the slope, finishing the sweep. I watched Pete out ahead of me, linking those perfect, effortless turns. It was such a pleasure to be in his presence, watching him eke out every ounce of joy no matter whether at work or play. And he would always do it with grace. There simply isn't a single thing I don't love about this guy. Secretly, in so many ways, I wanted to be like him.

About fifteen minutes after Pete had disappeared behind the column, he suddenly came out onto the fang about twenty feet up from the base. Carefully he swung his axes into the pillar, and delicately danced his feet around the column, tapping the front points of his crampons carefully into the tower.

"COOL!" I shouted out as I watched, completely mesmerized by what I was witnessing.

It was so odd. The binoculars gave me the illusion that I was right there with them, though I could not hear a single sound of their experience and there was no sound in the house. It was like watching action TV with the volume off.

Pete moved out to the face of the column, his back now to me. With each swing of an axe, he slowly made his way higher. Suddenly, to my complete astonishment, he stopped and put an anchor into the ice. I couldn't believe it.

I cried out, "Pete! No! What are you doing?"

Pete was by far the most experienced ice climber of the three of us. He knew better than that.

With his rope now clipped through the anchor in the ice, he moved on up. He was now about thirty-five feet up the column, and only ten feet from cresting its top and climbing onto the safety of a ledge.

Suddenly, a small puff of what looked like snow crystals filled the air around Pete, and, in disbelief, I watched a crack develop in the ice just a few feet above his ice axes. I saw the pillar settle slightly. The crack grew to about four inches wide, running horizontally across the entire width of the formation.

"Oh shit. NO!" was all I could mutter.

Momentarily, Pete stopped moving. Then, in a flurry of swings of his axes, he began to climb. He swung one axe above the crack and got it to stick. Just as his second axe drove into the ice, the entire formation parted from the wall.

Time moved in slow motion. With my mouth agape in absolute horror, and in perfect silence, I watched as the entire column started down. The ice began to disintegrate, and Pete fell to his left, then went completely upside down as he and the formation rocketed down the wall. About 130 feet down, Pete disappeared in a cloud of ice crystals as he and the entire formation impacted the lower angled part of the wall.

"NO!!!!!" I screamed out at the top of my lungs, as tears streamed down my face.

Seconds later, the remnants of the column tumbled down the wall and crashed into the base. As the cloud of ice disappeared, I saw Pete clearly, hanging from the end of the rope and an incredible amount of blood on the wall around him.

I ran out of the house toward my truck. I called Leah on my radio.

Through tears and shattered emotions I said, "Leah, there's been an accident. I need you to call 911. Tell them I think Pete is dead. I'm coming home to get my gear."

Two minutes later I was at the house and raced to grab my

equipment and dress for the conditions. Leah had called Doug's wife Sharon, and she arrived to come with me. I told her I thought Doug was probably all right, but I wasn't sure. She jumped in my truck and together we raced back down the canyon.

The trail to get up to the wall begins behind an electric power plant owned by Southern California Edison. I got on my radio and instructed all responders to meet at the plant. Minutes after Sharon and I got there, the ambulance arrived with two of Pete's medic colleagues, John Buccowich and Jim Endo. I asked them to sound the siren a few times to let Doug know we were aware of the accident and on our way. I told them that I was fairly certain that Pete was dead.

All of us were running on adrenaline, and hoping against hope that I was wrong -- that Pete was just seriously hurt. Together the four of us started the hike up through the snow in Doug and Pete's boot prints from earlier that morning.

My heart pounded out of my chest, and my lungs screamed for air as we pushed our bodies to the limit. We needed to ascend about 1,700 feet of steep snow to gain the base of the wall.

At the halfway point, I stopped to catch my breath. I looked up the wall. For a moment, in complete astonishment, I thought I saw Pete sitting up. Pulling off my sunglasses, which were running with sweat, I looked up again. Reality came crashing in. From this vantage it was clearly evident that Pete was in the same horizontal position at the end of the rope, and the blood was everywhere. Doug was at the belay, but we could see him moving.

John and I got out ahead of Jim and Sharon and closed in on the base of the wall. We managed to make voice contact with Doug, 400 feet above us. He let us know he was all right, but confirmed to us that Pete was gone.

As we reached the base of the wall, lying there among the remnants of the pillar, were Pete's gloves and ice axes. I swallowed hard, trying to keep my emotions in check. We needed to stay focused to assist Doug in any way we could.

A few minutes later, Jim and Sharon reached our position.

Above us, Doug made his way to Pete's body and secured it to the wall. He managed to piece together a section of shredded rope and began to rappel down to us.

Down below at the powerhouse, a crowd gathered as word of the accident spread throughout the county. I made radio contact with the SAR members who had arrived. They alerted me that the helicopter from Fallon was on the way. We formulated a plan. I would connect to a long line below the chopper and have them hold a hover while I clipped Pete's body off to me. Then we would fly back to the roadway at the power plant.

Not long thereafter, the chopper arrived. However, with the incoming storm bringing wind out of the west, the chopper was unable to hold a steady hover in the conditions, and the plan was scrapped. Recovering Pete's body would have to wait.

Nearly two hours after Pete's fall, Doug managed to make it to the base. He collapsed in a heap of emotions in Sharon's arms and could barely speak. With daylight fading, we made the gut-wrenching decision to go down before dark, while four hundred feet above us, our dear friend's body dangled from the mountain unattended.

Thirty minutes later, we arrived at the powerhouse and to a crowd of about seventy-five people, including Pete's wife. Doug and I were ushered into a waiting van. There we were met by a deputy and Russ Veenker, the acting Operations Leader for the SAR team. Our official SAR coordinator, Doug Magee, was in Mexico at the time. Together, Doug and I gave our statement as to what had happened. We also told them that it was our intention to go back up the wall the next day to recover Pete's body.

Russ looked us over, saw our emotions running thin, and made the decision to call in assistance from Yosemite Search and Rescue (YOSAR). We insisted that we were up to the task, but Russ felt he was justified in his decision.

As we exited the van the eyes of the crowd were on us, but we were in no mood to talk. We made the two-minute drive home to privacy. I came into the house almost in a trance. I headed straight for a hot shower. I was numb with grief.

After my shower, I sat down on the couch with Leah and the kids. My son Paden was almost five then, and daughter Micah was not quite two. Paden crawled into my lap.

"Did Torrey's daddy die?"

I looked back into his eyes, and with my voice barely audible, I said, "Yes. He did."

An hour later, with dinner done and the kids put to bed, I found myself back on the couch in Leah's arms. I couldn't hold it in any longer. I sobbed out the entire story to Leah.

Out on a mission, I stood up just fine. But once I was back around my family, I left the bravado behind, and my inner self showed through loud and clear. Like so many times in the past, Leah was the strength that allowed me to meet the adversities I faced on a regular basis. Knowing she was home with the kids allowed me to focus intently on completing the task and stay as safe as possible. Now, with the death of Pete, I needed her resilient faith and fervent prayers more than ever, to help me finish strong.

Knowing sleep would not come, I walked next door to Doug's house. Doug and Sharon had put their two boys to bed, and Russ was there, along with John Ellsworth. The phone rang non-stop, with everyone wanting to talk to Doug to find out what happened. Neither Doug nor Sharon was in any shape to talk with anyone, so I took phone duty. I kept the information to a minimum. No sooner would I hang up the phone, than it rang again. This went on for hours.

The last call I took was one I never wanted to answer. It was from Pete's Mom in LA.

"Dean. Hi, this is Kathy. I heard there was an accident and Pete was hurt. Is he ok?"

I felt ill, and paused for a second or two.

"He's gone, Kathy. I'm so sorry."

There was only silence, and then a faraway sounding voice.

"He's . . . gone. He's dead?"

"Yes. He took a long fall and was killed instantly. He didn't suffer at all. We will be going back tomorrow to get him down."

"He's still up there?" she shrieked in grief.

"Yes. We were unable to do the recovery today, but we'll get him down. I promise."

For what seemed like an eternity, I listened as she sobbed into the phone. When she was finished, she told me to hug Doug for her and that she would be on her way as soon as possible. We hung up. I wept quietly in the kitchen and decided to keep my conversation with Kathy to myself.

Completely spent and with nothing left for anyone, I lifted the phone off its base and set it on the counter.

Back in the living room, Russ, in soft tones, was explaining his reasons for having YOSAR come over to do the recovery. We shared our concerns that they would not get over to June Lake for at least another day, and with a storm coming in, Pete's body would likely be up on the wall for days, dangling for all the world to see like a grotesque tourist attraction. Doug, John and I insisted we could do the recovery, but Russ wouldn't budge. Not long after, Russ said goodnight and headed home.

It was near midnight, and we were exhausted, but our discussion continued. With Doug Magee in Mexico, Russ was our boss. Magee was deeply respected by all of us, and we knew that he valued our skills. We were certain that, if Magee had been around, he would never have made the decision Russ had. We also knew that if it were one of us up there, Pete would have been heading out at first light.

Two more friends showed up, Ed and Jane Escoto. They were devastated by the news of Pete's death, and wanted to help. Jim Endo arrived and was keen on assisting as well. For the next few hours we pored over our plan and assembled a gear list. We agreed to keep things on the low down and meet at the power plant at 5:00 a.m. We all headed home to prepare. Not one of us slept.

With my gear in my pack, I was out the door early. I got into my truck and turned my radio on to monitor the sheriff's department frequency. I suddenly heard the dispatcher's voice calling one of our deputies. That particular officer, Randy DesBaillet, was a good friend to all of us. He knew Pete as well.

I listened in disbelief as the dispatcher told Randy that the sheriff wanted him to proceed to the June Lake power plant to "intercept three loose cannons attempting the Schoerner recovery." I knew Randy had a twenty-five-minute drive to get to us, so as the others arrived, we moved quickly.

Ed, Jane, Jim and Sharon assisted with hauling gear, and the seven of us ascended the snow slope back to the base of the wall. I had my handheld radio in a harness on my chest, and continued to monitor the sheriff's frequency. Halfway up the slope, I heard Randy call dispatch upon his arrival and let them know that the "loose cannons" were already on their way up the mountain.

Weeks later, Randy told me "off the record" that he knew exactly who he would find at the power plant and how the bond was with climbers. He purposefully drove nice and slow to the call, giving us plenty of time.

As we approached the base of the wall, dawn revealed a heavily overcast sky. The wind swirled, lending an ominous feeling to an already challenging day. Together, we went over the plan once more.

Since he knew the route best, Doug would be the lead climber, fixing ropes as he went. John and I would follow, ascending the fixed lines with mechanical ascenders. Once we reached Pete's body, we would set up a series of anchors, then proceed to get the body in a body bag, which I had in my pack. We would then lower Pete's body 400 feet down the wall to the team at the base, then rappel back down ourselves.

One thing we were all certain of, we needed everything to go just right. We were breaking the law. The Sheriff's Department has jurisdiction over moving a body, and an official had already told us not to do the recovery. We were already going to be in enough trouble as it was. If one of us was hurt or killed in the process, there would be hell to pay. After a brief prayer for our safety and success, Doug started up the wall.

I was concerned about Doug. The climbing would not be easy. Much of the ice he and Pete had used to ascend this lower section of the wall had been destroyed by the avalanche of debris from the shattered pillar. I estimated the pillar likely consisted of twenty tons of ice. I secretly hoped that the more challenging climbing would force him to focus and keep his emotions about the loss of Pete in the background. As the sun rose, we saw he had made steady progress.

The continued chatter on the sheriff's frequency concerning our situation was also being monitored by others around the county. It wasn't long before a crowd gathered at the power plant. In a few hours, hundreds of people had arrived, watching our every move through binoculars. Once again we agreed, no foul ups.

An hour up the wall, Doug fixed the first rope, and John headed up, quickly ascending the line. He belayed Doug on the next pitch as I started up the first line. I took my time, careful to avoid chunks of ice that rained down as Doug made his way above. Not long after I reached John, Doug managed to get to a small, snow-covered ledge about fifty feet below Pete's body. He announced that he was going no further. He fixed the line, and John headed up. I followed John, hauling our first line with me as I ascended.

As I reached Doug and John on the ledge, it was clear Doug had come to an emotional end. He stated flat out that he was not going up to Pete's body. Without hesitating, John and I accepted that and formulated our plan.

John would lead up to Pete and set an anchor above the body. Doug and I would stomp out a small, relatively flat space in the snow on the ledge in order to lay out the body bag. I would then ascend John's fixed line up to Pete and clip the body off to myself. Then John would lower me to the ledge, and, with Doug's help, we'd get Pete's body in the bag. Doug stated he was good with that, and John began to climb. Below, the crowd grew.

After twenty minutes of cautious, tricky climbing, John found a spot about twenty feet above the body, and set a sound anchor. With the rope above now fixed, I attached my ascenders. Before leaving the ledge, I looked at Doug.

"Hey. Let's just get done what we need to do and get down, okay?"

He was clearly shattered but nodded in agreement. In a few short minutes, I arrived at Pete's body.

Years of SAR work had trained me well in dealing with death. As a way of coping, I told myself that a body was not a person; it was simply an object that needed to be removed from the environment for proper disposal. That may sound harsh in regard to someone's loved one, but the toll would be too great to bear if I made a personal connection. It was my mental survival mechanism. But now -- on this day -- it *was* personal. My profoundly handsome friend with the most infectious smile and a ready joke, hung lifeless before me.

Pete's body hung horizontally from a single anchor Doug had managed to fix to the wall. He was facing skyward, his arms and legs in unnatural positions and stiff with rigor mortis. His white helmet was still on, though clearly his skull had been shattered. Both of his eye sockets, nose and mouth were pooled with dark blood, and large icicles of blood and cranial spinal fluid (CSF) dangled from his jaw and ears. My heart pounded as I stared at my friend in utter disbelief. Once again the tears flowed. I closed my eyes and prayed silently.

"Lord God, I need your strength like never before. Shield us with your protection. Help us do our job, and wrap Pete's family in your loving arms."

I looked up at John above me. His face wore the same look as mine: a sorrow of unspeakable magnitude. I looked down to the power plant and the burgeoning crowd. Then I gazed up canyon towards the ski area, recalling that incomparable few minutes with Pete just days earlier. I took a few minutes to gather my emotions then looked back at John.

"Let's get this done."

I reached over and snapped off the grim icicles from Pete's head and cast them down the wall. I moved around Pete's body and clipped myself into the anchor he was hanging from then disconnected my ascenders from the line.

With my weight off the rope, John was able to haul up the slack and put me on belay. Facing the wall, I moved around the outside of Pete's body and secured his harness to mine with a couple of slings. With John holding all of our combined weight, I took out my knife and cut the sling Pete had been hanging from. His body was now essentially lying horizontally across my lap, and John slowly lowered us to the ledge. The smell of death was overwhelming.

In short order I arrived at the ledge, which was about three feet wide and perhaps eight feet long. Slowly, I eased Pete's body onto the bag. Within seconds, Doug began to sob uncontrollably.

"C'mon, Doug," I said softly, trying to calm him as I fought back my own emotions. "I know this is tough. Let's just do the job."

Unfortunately, Doug ended up being at Pete's head as we tried to tuck his rigid body into the bag.

Doug wept deeply, then suddenly bent down, put his face right in Pete's, and screamed at the top of his lungs. "Pete! You f****** asshole!!!!!" as he convulsed in sobs and tears.

Quickly, I reached across and grabbed Doug by the jacket. I pulled him to me and looked him directly in the eye.

"Hey! You need to get your shit together right now!!! Look down there!"

I nodded toward the valley below.

"There are hundreds of people down there with their eyes on us, including Pete's family! Let's just do our job the way Pete would have done for us, okay?!"

He stood back up.

"Just relax," I said. "Have some water. I've got this."

I finished tucking the body into the bag and zipped it closed.

I looked up at John and he asked, "What are you thinking?"

Though I really wanted to send Doug down, I felt it best to get Pete's body down first and keep Doug out of that duty. I called back up to John.

"How about I just keep the bag clipped off to me, and you lower me with the bag all the way to the base?"

John gave me a thumbs-up. I turned back to Doug.

"You okay with this plan?"

He seemed to have regained a bit of his composure.

"Sounds good," he said quietly.

I was now tied in to the end of a 400-foot line. I attached my ascenders to the line just above me then clipped off the sling from the body bag to the ascenders. The weight of Pete's body was then freed from my harness. I leaned back on the rope, and John lowered me. I guided the bag as it slid down the wall next to me.

Twenty minutes later, our base team was there to assist me as I reached the snow. An hour later, Doug and John rappelled the wall and were down safely. I got on my radio and called down to the team members in the crowd below, letting them know we were all down safely.

As we packed up our gear, we discussed the scene waiting for us at the power plant. Hundreds of people had gathered, including the entire SAR team and many Sheriff's Department personnel, including the sheriff himself, Dan Paranick. Many of Pete's colleagues from the fire department and medic staff were there as well, as was his family.

With our packs on, I kept a line tied to the body bag. I stayed behind to act as a brake, while Jim and Ed used another line to drag the bag down the snowfield. With hardly a word among us, the seven of us made our way down the mountain.

Forty minutes later, we reached the power plant. Waiting for us right where the snow met the parking lot, was the back end of the very ambulance Pete worked on. I disconnected my line from the bag and just sat down in the snow. Two of Pete's colleagues opened the rear doors of the ambulance, and pulled out the gurney. With tears streaming down their faces, they loaded Pete's body into the back of that ambulance. My dam finally broke. Waves of emotion poured out. I hung my head between my knees and let go.

We managed to exchange a few words with Cindy, Pete's wife, and she thanked us for our efforts.

Sheriff Paranick approached, "We'll be debriefing this event in the coming days. Go home and get some rest."

Others in the crowd could see the strain on our faces and, to their credit, just kept their distance. As the medic unit drove off with Pete's body, the crowd dispersed. Each of us headed home to begin the long task of recovery.

It was late afternoon, and my kids were napping when I arrived at the house. Leah greeted me, and tears flowed once more. I headed for a hot shower while she put dinner on the table.

We spent the evening together quietly, just enjoying playing with Paden and Micah on the floor, with me trying to choke back my emotions. The kids, so full of life, stood out in stark contrast to the shattered and drained feeling deep within my soul. Once Leah and I managed to get to bed, I lay awake, in spite of my exhaustion, tossing and turning.

At some point in the early morning hours, I drifted off, then suddenly bolted upright, soaked in sweat, having relived Pete's fall in a dream. But this was no dream. It was so terribly real. For the next four months I woke up this same way, over and over again. The dream always ended the same. Pete was gone.

The next morning, I received a call from Doug Magee. He had gotten word of Pete's death down in Mexico and had arrived home late the previous night. He wanted to speak with Doug, John and myself, so I agreed to meet at his home with the other guys.

Magee's wife Peggy had the coffee ready as we arrived, and both of them had plenty of hugs for all of us. This was clearly very tough on them, as well. They loved Pete like a son. As we sat down, we told the story from the beginning, not leaving out a single detail. We stood our ground with our decision to defy the sheriff and do what we knew Pete would have done. And Magee understood that. He told us that he would be meeting with the sheriff and Russ the following morning. Once that meeting was done, he said the sheriff would contact us for a meeting as well.

Later that day, I made my way over to Doug's place. For the first time since Pete's death, just the two of us talked together. I had some questions that only Doug could answer. I told him everything I had witnessed from the start then asked him to fill in the blanks.

Very slowly Doug poured out the story. Pete had told him over and over again that he wanted the lead on the pillar, so when they arrived at the belay spot, they set themselves up to do just that.

Then, Doug dropped a bombshell piece of information. As Pete was making his way up to the base of the pillar, one of the lenses of his glasses popped out and bounced down the cliff. In a fit of rage, he whipped the glasses off his face and tossed them off the wall. Pete's glasses were thick, and without them, he was as good as blind.

Doug said he would lead, but Pete wasn't having any of it. He charged on up to the pillar. As he climbed behind the pillar to search for placements for anchors in the rock, the shadow of the pillar compromised his vision even more. Pete was getting a real workout as he searched for an anchor. He grew frustrated and put a screw into the ice column. From my vantage I could not tell Pete had done this. Doug then lowered Pete off the screw and back to the base of the pillar for a rest.

Doug proceeded to tell Pete to untie from the line and pull the rope back through the ice screw, so that he would not be attached to the ice. But Pete refused. Doug told him if he didn't pull the rope through, he was going to take him off belay. Pete said, "Fine. I'll just solo the thing."

Pete's obsessive spirit had control of him. As experienced a climber as he was, his knowledge and wisdom were obliterated by his all-consuming determination to not be thwarted by his broken glasses. There was no way he was turning back at this point. He was leading that fang, and nothing would stop him. Without another word, he began to climb.

Thirty feet up the steep ice Pete got pumped again. He banged in what's known as a spectre, a special piece of ice protection that looks like a curved claw that can be put in faster than a screw. Once again, he clipped his rope to yet another anchor attached to the pillar instead of solid rock. Minutes later, as I had witnessed, the column shifted as the crack formed.

Pete never said a word. He just climbed furiously to get above the crack. When the formation collapsed, Doug plastered himself tight to the wall, turned his face away from the roar of the shattering tower, and held the belay line tight.

Suddenly, a tremendous pull on the line yanked Doug hard into the wall. When he finally looked down, all he could see was Pete dangling from the end of the line. The external sheath on the rope had been stripped open, exposing the inner strands of the rope's core. Incredibly, the rope had not snapped. Doug called down to Pete a few times, but it was obvious he was gone.

The next thing Doug remembered was hearing two blasts of the ambulance siren, then seeing us coming up to the base. He eventually got away from the belay and down to Pete. Then he tied Pete's body off. Using the undamaged portions of the rope, Doug spent the next few hours getting himself down.

As I took in the reality of these events, I began to understand Doug's outburst at Pete during the recovery. Doug was certain that Pete would have indeed untied from the rope and gone up the column solo, had Doug continued to challenge his judgment. It was Pete's unstoppable mindset that skewed his decision making, despite knowing better, and he had died because of it.

After what I had learned, I became angry with Pete as well. I simply could not fathom his decision. The grief from his choice crashed over the entire eastern-Sierra community like a tidal wave.

Over the next few days, Pete's family planned a memorial

service, and a viewing was held at the mortuary. I approached his casket. Pete was dressed in a set of mountain clothes, looking fresh and ready for another day on the ice. I thought I had no more tears to give, but once again they flowed down my face, as I looked upon my handsome friend for the last time.

Later that day, we received more disturbing news. At the meeting between the sheriff, Russ and Magee, the sheriff told Magee he wanted to bring the hammer down on Doug, John and me for violating his order. Magee argued that Russ had made the wrong decision.

"Had I been here," he told the sheriff, "there would have been three guys I would have chosen to do the recovery. And those are the three who did the job."

Unhappy that Magee refused to support Russ's decision, the Sheriff fired Magee.   We were appalled. Magee was the most respected SAR coordinator one could ever hope to work for. There simply wasn't anyone better at the job. His firing added misery to an already desperately miserable situation.

Being a little tightly wound, myself, I wrote a scathing letter to the Sheriff, leaving nothing left unsaid. In my opinion, firing Magee was a travesty. Russ was wrong to make the decision he had made, and, in spite of the "chain of command," I felt we did the right thing.

Magee took it all in stride. He and Peggy started spending most of their time at their place in Mexico, and, to his credit, Magee just let it go.

Sheriff Paranick ended up giving the three of us a verbal reprimand but thanked us for our service. Weeks later, Russ resigned from the team.

The week after Pete died, a packed-to-overflowing memorial service was held in the Mammoth Middle School gymnasium. With lights flashing, emergency vehicles from multiple counties paraded through Mammoth. Thousands of people braved the cold night, many holding candles, as we slowly passed.

Pete was a beloved member of the community, and his death

affected so many. Doug and I had a bronze plaque cast, which we bolted to the base of the wall below where Pete had left us. Years later, the new trauma center at Mammoth Hospital would be named in his honor.

I struggled with the decisions Pete had made that day. At times, I found myself angry with him. But that anger did not last. I focused on Pete's extraordinary life. Pete was no angel. He had his share of issues just like the rest of us. But his selfless acts of kindness toward perfect strangers inspired me to live the same way. I knew that I would never let anything get in the way of responding to a SAR call, because it was Pete's way. I wanted to be able to be counted on, just like Pete had shown me in his life.

With each SAR call that came in, I was reminded of how much I missed my friend. As the weeks passed, I battled a dark cloud of sadness and shattered emotions. The smell of winter was tinged with that awful scent of death. Spring could not come fast enough.

Pete left us at only forty years of age, and he left behind a wife and three amazing kids. I hope to someday be able to forget the way Pete died. But I will never forget the way he lived.

In memory of Pete Connelley Schoerner, September 1, 1955 -
January 29, 1996

CHAPTER 5

. . . we rejoice in our suffering,
because we know that suffering produces perseverance;
and perseverance, character; and character, hope.
And hope does not disappoint us,
because God has poured out His love into our hearts
by the Holy Spirit, whom He has given us.

Romans 5:3-5

March 1996
Northern Yosemite
High Sierra

A cold, winter wind blew steadily out of the west as the storm gathered power and energy from the Pacific. As the air mass slammed into the western flank of the Sierra Nevada, the moisture-laden clouds released their payload on the high country. The storm grew in intensity by the minute, and the flow continued toward the heart of the range. Snow fell like a thick paste as the initial surge of Pacific air rapidly cooled. Within hours, the sky billowed with wind-driven flakes the size of silver dollars, quickly adding to an already heavy snowpack in the high country. Over on the eastern flank of the range, at an altitude of 16,000 feet, a pilot steered his single engine plane westbound, straight into the teeth of the gathering storm.

June Lake, California
Eastern High Sierra

My lungs screamed and I took another deep breath of the cold winter air, as I labored with a snow shovel on my driveway. I should have been inside near the roaring wood stove, nursing the bronchitis that had kept me home from work. But I thought perhaps a good dose of cold air would help loosen things up in my chest. Snow fell heavily as the afternoon progressed, and I wanted to keep up with the task. After laboring for an hour, I finally gave in to the aches and headed inside.

I whined to Leah, secretly hoping for a little sympathy. There would be none today. She reminded me that it was my choice to go ice climbing earlier in the week when I wasn't feeling totally up to it, which undoubtedly led to my current state.

I had needed to get out though, for my own mental health. It had been a little over a month since I'd watched Pete die, and the aftermath had left me searching. I needed to get my head back in the game. I wasn't sleeping well, with the constant nightmare of Pete's fall replayed over and over in my dreams. It always ended the same, waking me up to the reality that he was gone.

I needed a diversion, something that smelled of life, not death. The phone rang late that afternoon, bringing news that I didn't really need to hear. Somewhere out in the gathering whiteout a plane was down.

Leah could only stare in disbelief and voice her disdain for my decision to go out with the rescue team to search for this plane. I knew deep down that I was not in the best condition to be out in the cold, but something inside me said go. I thought about Pete and his willingness to serve at any time. If he were here, in these same circumstances, he'd be headed out the door.

I gathered my winter gear, kissed Leah and the kids, and jumped in my truck. As I made my way out of town through the heavy snow, I desperately hoped we could find this plane with survivors. I needed it for my soul. As I drove through the intensifying storm, the odds did not look good.

I arrived at our operations base at the firehouse in the small town of Lee Vining. There I was met by other team members along with a few Sheriff's department personnel. We pored over the information that we had so far.

What we knew was that at approximately 1:00 p.m., Oakland Air Traffic Control (OATC) had been in contact with a single engine Beechcraft Bonanza aircraft flying westbound. The pilot and sole occupant, Jamie Cox, reported that he had lost his engine over Northern Yosemite. His visibility was zero in the swirling snow, and he was losing altitude rapidly. Oakland Air gave him a vector to Lee Vining Airport, a tiny landing strip for small planes. Jamie had made a northerly U-turn and glided back east. With the wind now behind him, Oakland Air had him on radar at over 140 knots. A few minutes later, the plane disappeared from the scope.

OATC had provided us with the current satellite "hits" from the plane's emergency locator transmitter (ELT). These special transmitters send out a beacon from the aircraft upon impact. Meanwhile, as satellites travel overhead, the receiver beacon the satellites send out travels to earth in a conical shape. By the time that signal reaches earth from such great height, the diameter of the cone encompasses a large area. Once a general area is identified by the satellite, a more accurate location requires ELT monitoring from a low-flying aircraft. To get that, we would need better weather conditions.

As darkness approached and the storm intensified, it was apparent we were in for a long wait. We could only hope that wherever Jamie Cox came down, he came in soft and was alive and well in the plane. He was going to need a lot of luck. If the crash hadn't killed him, the worsening conditions certainly could.

By 10:00 p.m. I was heading home, saddened that we could do nothing for Jamie at the moment and, at the same time, relieved that I was headed back to a warm bed and much-needed rehab. My lungs were on fire, and my throat was raspy. I needed my health back to be effective in what was likely going to be a long, tiring, and dangerous search.

Dawn on day two did not look good. Two feet of snow had

fallen on my driveway overnight, and it was still coming down. Most likely, the high country where Jamie's plane had gone down had received twice that much. There would be no flyovers today; the cloud ceiling was too low, and the heavy snow just too thick. Any ground effort would be suicide in the high avalanche danger. We kept our air resources on standby, and watched the sky.

As we entered day three, it continued to snow, but the intensity was waning. We had picked up another few feet but experienced occasional breaks in the storm. With the slightly better conditions, an Air Force C-130 executed some flyovers to try to pick up the ELT signal. They were successful with five separate hits on their scope, all within about six miles of each other.

This sporadic nature of the locations is common in the kind of elements we were dealing with. The ELT signal can bounce off formations like peaks and valleys, as well as snow fields. We would need even closer surveillance to pinpoint the location, and that meant helicopters and ground personnel. It also meant one more day of waiting. Jamie's chances were getting slimmer with each passing hour.

I was out the door at 6:00 a.m. on day four. I headed for our new operations center, located at the Ranger Station in Lee Vining Canyon. My health was slightly better, though my lungs still ached in the cold air, and my voice was all but gone.

The weather, however, was looking considerably better. It was still snowing lightly, but the forecast was for clearing by late morning. The avalanche conditions remained extreme. If we were going in to look for the plane, we would have to use extreme caution.

Upon arrival at SAR base, we were introduced to Jamie's father, who had come from out of state to assist in any way he could. I could only imagine what he was going through, not knowing anything of his son's whereabouts or condition and fearing the worst.

As we formulated our plan, Mr. Cox eased the tension we all

felt by saying, "My son may either have come down soft and is holed up in the plane trying to survive, or he flew into a rock in the sky."

It was clear he was prepared for whatever the outcome. We needed to be, too, but we hoped to find a living human being who would be very cold and in need of good care.

Utilizing the information the aircraft had gathered the past few days, we narrowed our search area to a region of high probability. From a few areas along the highway here in the canyon, we had been able to pick up a weak ELT signal with a hand-held locator. This device looks like a small radio with a TV antenna attached. We moved the array back and forth to hone in on the direction from which the signal was coming. When the signal is located, the transceiver gives out an audible tone. That tone was almost a sure sign that the plane was down on the east side of the crest. It was time to go.

A team of four was selected based on availability, backcountry experience, fitness, and a willingness to suffer. Gary Guenther had been a member of the SAR team for many years. His years as a ranger with the Forest Service had made him an expert on backcountry travel, with firsthand knowledge of our search area. He was also a certified avalanche forecaster and expert backcountry skier. Though the years had added a few pounds to his frame, Gary was up for the challenge, and would be a key part of our team.

Karl Chang volunteered for this mission straight away. He had been a candidate member of the SAR team for a while. Only his busy schedule had kept him from making it through all of the required trainings for acceptance as a full member. As a biologist for the Department of Fish and Game, Karl's area of expertise was tracking beacon-clad wildlife in the backcountry. His many years following mountain lion and bighorn sheep made him an expert with the ELT system. He was also extremely fit, and he was well versed in operating in avalanche-prone terrain.

Pete DeGeorge was a brand new candidate to the team.

Though I was hesitant to bring him along due to his lack of backcountry experience, he was eager, and physically fit. He was also agreeable to the fact that this mission would likely involve at least one night out on bivouac in sub-zero temperatures.

The four of us loaded into the Sheriff's department snow-cat for the long ride up to the base of Lee Vining Peak where our ground search would begin. Along with our personal gear, we carried charcoal-fired heat packs that we would need to warm Jamie, should we find him in a serious hypothermic state. As we rumbled up the mountain, I gulped throat lozenges and secretly wondered if I were up to the task. After the first hour of the cat ride, I was certain I was good to go.

Helicopters from three different agencies were already flying search patterns in the area. We needed to be in there to utilize the hand-held locator, which would be the most accurate.

After an hour and a half, we arrived at the Boy Scout camp near the foot of the peak. The buildings of the camp were buried by ten feet of new snow. The snow-cat could go no further. We strapped into our snowshoes, shouldered our packs, and headed toward the peak.

Breaking trail in the deep snow was daunting. Even with very large snowshoes on, we sank up to our thighs in the fresh powder. Our packs bulged at nearly fifty pounds, loaded with overnight gear, assorted medical equipment, food and water.

Because we were traveling in an area of extreme avalanche danger, we all wore avalanche beacons. These small transceivers would send out a signal that could be detected should one of us be buried in snow. The other team members would switch their transceivers to the receive mode, and begin searching for the buried partner. This must be done quickly, as the victim may have suffered injury or be unable to breathe. We were all familiar with the procedure and chose our line of ascent carefully to minimize the danger.

The weather improved steadily, though it remained bitterly cold. The snowfall had abated and visibility was excellent. Every quarter of a mile, we stopped to take another bearing with the ELT wand and fix a new position to hike toward. After a few hours of difficult trudging, it was apparent that the plane was, indeed, in the vicinity of Lee Vining Peak.

As we approached the eastern flank of the summit, our ELT signal grew very strong. The helicopters were searching an area about half a mile north of our position, but our signal here on the ground was more south and west. It was now late afternoon, about 3:30. We had reached a small plateau area about 1,000 feet below the summit. As we entered the peak's shadow, the temperature plummeted.

We followed the ELT signal in a southwesterly heading and came to a large, open area, completely devoid of trees. Looking up at the peak, it was easy to see that if the snow above us avalanched, it would come down this path, and it likely had many times in the past. One at a time, we dashed across this "run out" path that an avalanche would take. Once across, our ELT signal grew ever stronger.

I radioed one of the helicopters to come back down to our position and begin searching the area between us and the summit of the peak. Our altimeters showed that we were at 11,000 feet. The cold was intense, and standing still was not an option. My lungs were on fire from six hours of labored breathing in the brutally cold air, and my voice was barely audible. My thighs screamed in pain from miles of snowshoeing in deep conditions. We were all ready for a break. It would be dark in a few hours, and I relished the thought of digging a snow cave and hunkering down for the night. Then the radio crackled.

The helicopter crew had been flying orbits around the summit of the peak, and spotted the aircraft just 1,200 feet above our position. I was instantly re-energized. We ascended the eastern flank of the peak towards the summit in the safest direct line to the hovering chopper.

After climbing the first 500 feet, I spotted the aircraft. In the shadowed conditions, we simply had not been able to see it from our vantage. The plane was white as well, with only a small blue stripe on its side to discern it from the snow. My adrenaline flowed at the thought of getting to Jamie in a matter of minutes, and I quickly left my teammates far behind.

As I approached the aircraft from the downhill side, my heart sank. The plane was lying upside down, with the prop, engine, control panel and cockpit completely blown away. I managed to shout out Jamie's name, with no response. As I moved around the front of the cabin and came to the uphill side of the plane, I realized our worst fears.

Jamie was hanging upside down from the seat belt, his body frozen in a horrific, contorted position. Dressed only in jeans and a t-shirt at the time of the crash, his body had instantly been exposed to the cold. The goose bumps on his skin were the largest I had ever seen, almost the size of peas, and they were frozen in place, adding to the macabre scene. He had suffered tremendous fractures of his extremities, with one arm curled into a horrible circle, and frozen in a clump near his neck. His left leg had been snapped at the knee, with the lower leg bent the opposite way the knee normally bends, putting his foot right in his face. And he had been decapitated at the eyebrows.

Over the years, these air crash victims were always the most horrible of sights, but to see a body frozen solid into such a ghastly position was almost beyond belief. I sank down in the snow and said a prayer for his father. I could not bring myself to radio in and confirm to SAR base that Jamie was dead. Just a few weeks prior I had to tell Pete's Mom that he was gone. I didn't want to be the bearer of the bad news again. I decided to wait for the rest of my team to arrive. I knew Jamie did not suffer. His death had been immediate.

Pulling off my pack, I reached for a water bottle and sat down in the snow to try to get my voice back to working order. The water was frozen solid. I checked the thermometer I had hanging from my parka; it read twenty-three degrees below zero.

The terrain at the wreck site was steep, so I stomped out a

platform with my snowshoes so that the other guys would have a place to drop their packs. As they arrived one by one, they saw the body and just sank down in the snow and stared, out of breath and at a loss for words. When your hopes are for finding a live victim, death seems all the more cruel. Gary radioed down that we were all at the aircraft, that Jamie was deceased, and that we would be getting to work on extricating his body.

I grabbed a long sling from my pack, climbed off our platform, and made my way to Jamie's body. Because the plane was inverted, the body was suspended above the snow, hanging from the lap belt of the seat. His waist had folded over the latch of the belt, and then his body had frozen solid, making getting to the latch impossible. I pulled out my knife and cut the belt on either side of the seat, dropping the body into the snow. I secured the sling around his waist and threw the other end up to the guys. Together we hauled the body to our little platform.

With the extrication complete, the next task was to get the body to a reasonable landing zone for the chopper. A few hundred yards to the south of our position was a large flat area, big enough to accommodate the Army Blackhawk, a ship that was capable of landing in those conditions at nearly 12,000 feet.

Moving the body across the slope proved to be a daunting task given the angle of the terrain, the fatigue in our bodies, and the numbing cold. However, the exertion did provide a welcomed measure of warmth.

Unfortunately, the helo had to return to Mammoth Airport for fuel, so we were in for a bit of a wait. As the sun sank lower in the west, we put on every bit of clothing we had. Finally, after an hour and a half, the chopper returned. As they made their approach, I radioed them and asked if the crew could have a body bag available for us in the chopper. They confirmed that request and started their approach.

As the Blackhawk came in for a landing, the rotor wash created a mind-numbing wind chill. The pilot needed to keep the engines at full throttle in the cold conditions, so we tried to work quickly to get the body into the bag. With the bizarre position the body had frozen in, we were unable to get it in the bag.

I was concerned that Mr. Cox would be at the airport waiting for his son's body to arrive, so I was adamant that we get it in the bag. No parent should ever have to see their child in such a condition. We had dealt with rigor mortise in bodies countless times and had been successful in bending the bodies enough to get them inside body bags. But this body was frozen hard as a rock.

We lifted the body onto the floor of the chopper. Screaming as loud as I could over the roar of the engines, I had a couple of the crew members sit on top of the torso. The rest of us got a firm hold on the legs and lower torso and tried to flex the body flat.

Suddenly, we were all sent sprawling, with me flying headfirst out of the chopper, as the body literally snapped in two at the waist. For a few seconds we just stared at each other with mouths agape, as if we were children guilty of breaking a treasured vase. Seconds later, we burst into an insane, nervous laughter. None of us had ever witnessed anything quite so surreal.

Now in two pieces, the body was quickly bagged, and we cleared away from the helicopter. With a roar and a wicked blast of stinging snow, the chopper lifted off and disappeared in the waning, blue light.

Now brutally cold and anxious to get off the mountain, we donned our packs, picked the safest line down the peak, and went full speed in hopes of getting some warmth back into ourselves. Thankful for a downhill dash after going up all day, we arrived back at the Boy Scout camp in a few hours and loaded back into the snow-cat for the long ride back to SAR base.

Upon our arrival, we learned that Mr. Cox had left for home as soon as he was told of his son's death. How I wished that we could have had a better outcome. I was relieved that I did not have to face Mr. Cox and give him any details.

We were all tired, and my lungs and throat ached. My voice had disappeared as well. We headed for a local restaurant for some much-needed hot food and a debriefing. Poring over the details of the day, we were grateful we had accomplished an exhausting and grim task without further incident. We went home disappointed that we had not saved a life, but knowing Jamie's family would have closure about his death. That would be our consolation.

I walked through our door at nearly 11:00 p.m., completely hoarse, and ready for a hot shower and a good night's sleep. Lying in bed, wrapped in Leah's arms, I thought back on the previous four months. Four body recoveries in as many months had left me weary. I felt like I had aged years. The heartache of losing Pete just wouldn't leave, and Jamie's horrible death brought it all back again.

I was desperately ready for spring to arrive and replace the smell of cold winter days that had become tinged with the scent of death.

Only with the warming days of spring did I begin to rejoice again in the beautiful surroundings that I was so privileged to call home. As the aspens burst forth their crop of leaves, and the birds returned to the air, so were my joy and peace rekindled and serenity returned to my spirit.

Once again, God's word was manifest to me through events in my life. Persevering through the difficult times had produced the ability to deal with events that otherwise would overwhelm. God's faithfulness to "never leave or forsake me" allowed me the strength to provide a service to Jamie's family and to come out of a difficult winter of death with a hope and a yearning for the future.

Note: The name "Jamie Cox" is a pseudonym, used out of respect and privacy for the family of the deceased.

CHAPTER 6

The Lord is near to all who call upon Him,
to all who call on Him in truth.

Psalm 145:18

In February of 1945, American Marines found themselves embroiled in what would turn out to be one of the most brutal battles of the Pacific Theater in World War II: the battle for the tiny island of Iwo Jima. It was here, in the midst of utter destruction and death that one man was in the right place at the right time.

Joe Rosenthal, an unassuming wire-service photographer covering the battle for the Associated Press, scrambled to the rocky summit of Mt. Suribachi, the island's lofty high point. Aiming his camera at six men struggling with a length of pipe, Rosenthal bracketed perhaps the most reproduced image of all time: the raising of the Stars and Stripes on that volcanic summit.

That single photograph became one of the greatest morale boosters for both soldiers and civilians alike and increased the sale of war bonds exponentially. The momentum of the war shifted dramatically after Iwo Jima fell, and, in August of that year, Japan surrendered.

In his book, *Flags of our Fathers,* author James Bradley recounts the efforts of those six men who raised the flag that day, one of whom was his father. Three of the six would not live through the battle. But they did not consider themselves to be heroes. From the testimony of the survivors, it was clear that all of them were simply doing their jobs. They had been ordered to raise a flag on that summit, and they succeeded. Standing nearby was scrappy Joe Rosenthal, in the right place at the right time.

August 8, 1998

I sat at the drawing table in my home office and stared blankly at the pattern of lines I had drawn and which represented my vision for the floor plan of our future home. Though not overly complicated, the challenge was to locate the walls such that they supported the huge roof system that dominated my design for the home, while keeping an interesting and usable floor plan. All aspects had to come together to create a finished product that both Leah and the children would be happy with.

The phone rang, but I stayed in my chair in hopes that my evening with the house plans would not be interrupted. I heard Leah answer the phone downstairs, and in seconds, my seven-year-old son, Paden, bounded into the office with the handset. He handed me the phone. "Mom says it's the Sheriff."

The Watch Commander informed me that a hiker was at the trailhead just half a mile from our home and had some information about an injured climber high in the backcountry. A few minutes later, a deputy arrived at the house with a note the hiker had carried out. The note was written that morning and read as follows:

> *Mt. Rescue Unit:*
> *We have in our care a climber we encountered who was injured on Banner Peak. His condition requires helicopter evacuation due to right hip and right knee injuries. Location is the North Shore of Thousand Island Lake about one mile from the outlet. Look for yellow tarp on rocks.*
> *Bruce Meyer, M.D. Ret.*
> *Orthopedic Surgery*

My first reaction to the note was, "Wow, this injured guy is the luckiest guy on the planet!" Not only did some hikers come to his aid, but one of them is a bone specialist! Clearly, the victim was in good hands. The good doctor was also thorough in his briefing in regards to injuries and location, and his assessment of the necessity of an air evacuation was correct. Thousand Island Lake was a stiff hike of nearly ten miles from the trailhead. Wheeling the injured man out in a litter was out of the question.

The sun had been down for an hour, so it was clear this would be a "first light" operation the following morning. Having this kind of time to prepare for a rescue is rare, and I was thankful for the opportunity. I plotted the location and gave the coordinates to the Watch Commander, who then relayed that information to the helicopter crew at the Naval Air Station at Fallon. We were all set for 7:00 the next morning, and I once again got comfortable for the evening with my house plans.

I got going early, packing and dressing for the mountains, just in case something happened with the availability of the helo. I made the half-mile drive to the June Mountain Ski Area parking lot, our chosen base of operations and ideal landing zone for the helicopter. In a few minutes I had the area roped off with caution tape, as additional team members arrived. As we waited for the chopper, our ground team was established, and performed an equipment check. We were ready, should the helo get turned around.

At 7:00 a.m., the chopper appeared overhead. When we made radio contact, I immediately recognized the familiar voice of Lt. Jay Van Cleve, the pilot for the day's mission. I had flown many missions with Lt. Van Cleve. He was one of the best. Things were just getting better for this injured climber.

Lt. Van Cleve kept the chopper in the air, while we verified the victim's coordinates, told the helo team we would have the medic ambulance waiting for their arrival, and wished them good luck. Minutes later, the chopper disappeared over the ridge and into the high country.

Jay was piloting the venerable Bell UH-1 Iroquois. Developed by Bell Helicopter in the late '50s, this ship proved its mettle in Southeast Asia during the Viet Nam war. Its original designation was the HU-1, where it got its nickname, "Huey."

Whenever we needed an air resource, the Huey was my ship of choice, mainly for its hoist capability. We could winch victims into the helo while holding a hover. More than that, the crews trained with us routinely and are top-notch professionals.

Less than half an hour after heading into the high country the ship returned with its grateful cargo, and the medics carted the victim off to the hospital. Another successful mission was complete, and we didn't even have to break a sweat.

As was customary with our team, we offered to take the Navy crew of five out to a local restaurant, and they eagerly accepted. They locked down the ship and we drove into town.

At the restaurant, I sat down next to Jay. It had been awhile since I'd seen him, and I was anxious to catch up.

"Can't tell you how glad I am to see you, Dude," I said. "How's your family?"

"Everyone's good. Thanks. Kids are driving my wife nuts, but we're having a blast with them."

"Yep," I agreed. "They can be a handful. Wait till they're teenagers, my friend. You've got a real eye-opener coming."

"Oh, man, don't I know it," Jay said with a big smile. "I remember myself at that age. Poor Mom and Dad."

"So, have you guys been flying a lot of missions lately," I inquired.

"Yep. Typical summer. And lots of Navy stuff on top of all the civilian issues, so we've been hoppin'."

"Anything noteworthy, or just haul-outs like today's mission?" I asked.

"Today was pretty much a carbon copy of what we've been seeing," he said. "Fly in, grab 'em, fly out. No big deal. Today was as easy as it gets."

I smiled at my friend. "Well, stick around, because the next one is likely to be a bit more exciting."

Not thirty seconds later, my cell phone rang. The call was,

indeed, the Watch Commander. I snapped at the other SAR personnel at the table to quiet down. A subject with a broken leg was reportedly yelling for help near the base of the north face of North Peak, near the top of Tioga Pass at about 10,000 feet. I relayed the information to everyone present.

"Well that doesn't sound too bad," Jay said.

"Yah," I replied. "Sounds simple, but we've done a ton of operations in that area, and every one of them was a whole lot worse that the initial report.

"We could really use you guys on this one, if you can refuel and meet us at North Peak."

"I'll have to contact the C.O. and clear the mission," he said, "but I'm pretty sure we'll be able help out."

We all jumped up from the table, just as food was arriving; breakfast would have to wait. A few team members drove the crew back to the chopper. The rest of us got in our vehicles and sped toward the trailhead at Saddlebag Lake, twenty minutes away.

North Peak is a stunning crag that sits on the northern border of Yosemite National Park and our county of Mono. At 12,242 feet, it's not overly high yet is a much coveted summit to gain. The attraction is largely due to its easy access from the trailhead: only a mile and a half of nearly flat trail walking to gain its lower slopes. The crew at the Saddlebag Lake Resort even offers water-taxi service, making the approach to the peak all the more attractive. The mountain presents routes from all aspects, with most being in the non-technical range of difficulty.

The north face is home to three prominent couloirs -- steep, narrow gullies or crevasses, often choked with snow or ice -- all of which see a fair amount of traffic by climbers throughout the summer and fall months. It is here where most of our operations on the mountain have taken place, and more than likely where we were heading on this sunny August morning.

I raced up Tioga Pass on 120 West toward the trailhead, curving and careening through some of the most scenic landscape

of the entire Sierra Nevada. I radioed the Inyo Forest Service for
more information. I was told the call had come in from one of
their backcountry rangers, Leslie, who had heard shouting
coming down the mountain. She had relayed the information on
her handheld radio. I was given Leslie's call sign so I could contact
her once I arrived at the lake.

Following close behind me in his vehicle was fellow SAR
member Joe Rousek. If I had the entire roster of personnel from
our team to pick from for this mission, Joe would have been my
choice. Like me, Joe came to SAR with an extensive climbing
background. He was in good physical condition, had all of his gear
with him and was always eager to get into the mountains. Not
only had I climbed with Joe over the years, I also knew him as a
member of my church. Together, physically and spiritually, Joe
and I made a strong team.

I arrived at Saddlebag Lake and drove directly to the water
taxi at the marina. Richard Ernst, the owner of the resort, met me
there. He and his wife, Carmen, had served our team on many
occasions over the years, providing not only water-taxi service
but also incredible meals both during and after missions in the
area. They were a huge resource, assisting in saving many lives
and were aware of the present situation.

I radioed Leslie on the other side of the lake, and she gave us a
bit more information. Apparently, a man had attempted to ski one
of the couloirs on the north face and had taken a fall. A couple of
hikers had witnessed the fall from below and were with the
victim at the base of the couloir. They had indicated that the
victim's leg was broken.

I had climbed this particular couloir on a number of occasions,
so I knew we would have a fair bit of scrambling and snowfield
climbing to reach the location. Joe arrived, and as we donned
harnesses, I briefed him with the information we had. Together
we quickly assembled the gear we thought we would need and
loaded into Richard's boat. Another SAR member arrived and
took over the duty of rescue-base operations and radio relay.

Then Joe and I set out across the lake.

We carried everything we would need for a technical ice and snow rescue: ropes, ice screws, ice axes and crampons, assorted medical gear, and radio communications equipment. As the boat skipped across the water, I strained to listen for the comforting sound of the helicopter.

The five-minute boat ride brought us to the north shore and the start of our mile-and-a-half dash to the scene. We left the luxury of the trail after a few hundred yards and headed overland through boulder fields, skirting small alpine lakes, in a direct line to the base of the peak. We spotted three people near the base of the couloir, 500 vertical feet above us. As we neared steeper ground, we heard what we had been openly praying for: the familiar thump-thump of an approaching helicopter. As the chopper came into view I radioed Jay.

"Jay, look for the party of three near the base of the eastern-most couloir."

On their second pass, they spotted the scene.

"We'll attempt a landing on the glacier 500 feet above the location of the victim," Jay responded. "It looks like the only LZ on this side of the mountain. If we can set down, I'll send our medic and two other crew members down to the scene on foot."

A radio call from SAR base informed Joe and me that the team was on the way in with additional gear and personnel. We instructed them to follow the same route we took to reach the scene and to contact us when they got closer, so we could direct them accordingly.

The chopper set down on the glacier just as Joe and I reached the steeper terrain, 500 feet below the victim. We ascended a forty-five-degree rock wall and carefully worked our way around dangerous sections streaming with fast moving melt-water. Fortunately, we were both experienced enough to climb un-roped, thereby saving precious time.

The Navy crew was nearly 1,000 feet above us, and we watched as they made their way down to the scene. At one point, I had to radio them to be careful. In their haste they were inadvertently knocking loose incredible rock-fall, some of which almost took Joe and me right off the wall.

About 250 feet below the scene, our rock wall turned into a steep snowfield. Here the snow was soft enough that we could forgo the crampons, spikes strapped to our climbing boots that allow traction on hard snow and ice.

As I stopped to catch my breath, I was able to make voice contact with the subjects at the scene: two men and a woman. They informed me that the victim was trapped in a crevasse -- a deep crack in the ice -- and was in a bad way. The woman on the scene was the victim's wife, Jessica. Just then, the Navy boys arrived and assessed the situation.

Joe and I were getting pretty worked with the effort of climbing up to the location. At over 11,000 feet we were carrying hefty loads. The sky was clear, and in spite of the altitude and relatively early hour, the snowfield baked in the morning sun.

I stopped to clear the sweat from my sunglasses and saw Joe a few hundred feet below. Suddenly, I heard a blood-curdling scream from a female voice above me, followed immediately by the desperate voice of Wade McConnell, the Navy medic. "Dean! Get up here! We need your help!"

My adrenaline spiked. I put my chin on my chest and pumped my legs up the snowfield like a man possessed. White lights burst in my vision, as my body searched for oxygen. Wade continued to shout down information as I climbed.

"Dean! He is down in a crevasse and has just gone into full arrest! We think he may have a spinal injury, and we can't get down to him!"

In a furious burst, I managed the last few feet of the climb and arrived at the scene, completely unable to speak a word as my chest heaved in search of every breath. I tossed off my pack, got down on my chest, and peered into the crevasse.

The victim, Erik Schultz, was indeed about seven feet down in the shoulder wide crevasse, lying on his back, his eyes fixed and dilated.

A large boulder three times the size of my truck bordered the crevasse. When Erik had come flying out of the mouth of the couloir, his body slammed into this boulder. His helmet lay nearby, shattered like an eggshell.

Erik not being able to feel his body was a sure sign of spinal damage. Clearly, there was no way to get a backboard under him, or a neck brace on him, considering the cramped quarters of the crevasse. Now, with his heart and breathing stopped, the spinal injury was the least of our concerns.

"We need to get him out, NOW!" I managed to yell out, my lungs still gasping for breath. Together, four of us lay down on the snow, reached deep into the crevasse, and managed to grab Erik's clothing and the harness he was wearing. With a mighty heave, we extricated him from the crevasse and onto a reasonably level spot between the crevasse and the giant boulder.

Navy crewman Nick Wiscons and I immediately started CPR, while Jessica screamed at the top of her lungs. Wade attempted an I.V. while the other crewman went back up towards the helo to find the bottle of oxygen they had dropped on their way down.

The scene was desperate. I needed to communicate with our rescue base as well as with Jay in the helo to give them a status report, but the task of CPR kept me from using my radio, which was in a harness on my chest. I needed Joe, my SAR teammate, on the scene badly. Looking down the slope I saw him closing in. I knew his lungs were on fire like my own, but I yelled down to him anyway.

"Joe! I need you up here . . . NOW!!!!"

Wade managed to get the I.V. in, and we saw the other crewman making his way back with the 02 bottle. Jessica was still screaming. Though she was watching her husband die, in a moment of tension, I yelled at her.

"Jessica! I need you to stop screaming! Get over here and call out to Erik. Talk to him. Help him stay with us."

Nick and I had been doing CPR for a couple of minutes when

Joe arrived. He climbed onto the adjacent boulder and saw us performing CPR on Erik's ashen body. Joe threw his arms in the air, his head back, and between gasps of air cried out, "Lord! God!"

Tears welled up in my eyes as I witnessed Joe's desperate prayer. I pushed hard on Erik's chest. Joe dropped his pack and immediately got on the radio and relayed our circumstances to the rest of the team and the chopper. He advised the other team members to hold in position at the base of the peak until we needed them. We had to get Erik on that chopper if he were going to survive.

Suddenly, amidst the chaos, Erik's abdominal muscles shuddered. We stopped CPR and checked his pulse; we had a heartbeat. I continued to administer breaths to Erik while Nick helped get the O2 bottle and mask hooked up and oxygen flowing into his mouth and nose. Within minutes of Erik's heart starting, he began to take very shallow breaths on his own. With more tears flowing down my face, I kept up with rescue breathing as Joe called for the helo.

Our plan was for the chopper to hover directly above us, lower down the winch cable, and haul Erik and Wade up in the litter together.

Jay had kept the chopper running on the glacier above us the entire time, and we heard him throttle up and lift into a hover. Within minutes he had approached our position.

Though his eyes were still fixed and dilated, the color was returning to Erik's skin. He was trying to breathe on his own, but I continued using the intubation bottle to rescue breathe for him. As the helo approached, we prepared to operate within the extreme noise and wind of the rotor wash.

Jay radioed down, "Between the altitude and the warm temperatures, we're at maximum power capability for the helo. Be prepared for a potential wave off."

In terms of working with helicopters, the warmer the air and the higher the altitude, the thinner the air that is holding the ship aloft. Also, wind comes off Sierra peaks erratically. Moving the chopper even a hundred feet can change the dynamic dramatically.

The pilot needs a direction to steer the helo should things go wrong, known as a wave off. In this particular case, we were right up against a vertical cliff face, and the loss of any ability to hold a stable hover could be disastrous for the ship, the crew and all of us beneath the helo. Should a problem arise, Jay would immediately dive the chopper straight off the side of the cliff to gain air speed. A wave off in this situation would mean carrying Erik out, which he would surely not survive.

As the bird approached, we instructed Jessica and the two other hikers who had come up with her to get into protected positions amongst the boulders. This chopper has a forty-eight-foot rotor diameter, and we were no more than fifty feet from the base of the cliff, so the margin of error was tight.

Joe radioed down our plan to both the team members waiting below, as well as to our rescue base. He also advised them to get word to the hospital in Mammoth that Erik was likely going to need a Care Flight to a major trauma center in Reno.

Carefully, we secured Erik to a backboard then strapped him into the rescue litter, as Jay eased the ship into a hover twenty-five feet above our heads. The crew chief standing in the open doorway called out directions for Jay, as he focused on the ship's gauges and attitude. The winch cable was lowered and we secured it to the litter. Wade clipped himself into the cable, and we piled the O2 bottle into the litter. Once he was secured, I handed the intubation bottle over to Wade, and he continued to rescue breathe for Erik.

I looked up at the helo. I gasped as I saw how dangerously close the tail rotor was getting to the cliff. I waved at the crew chief in the doorway to get his attention and gestured wildly at the tail. He had been concentrating on the winch cable, watching for Wade's signal to begin hauling. He noticed me, took one look at the tail, and called into his microphone to Jay. Quickly, the tail swung away from the cliff and the chief and I exchanged a thumbs-up.

Wade gave the signal to haul, and the litter was quickly hauled up and into the ship. With Erik and Wade now safely aboard, Jay carefully eased the ship sideways and away from the cliff, then quickly dove down into the valley below. Within seconds, the roar of the rotors and jet engines was replaced by the pristine silence of the mountains.

Jessica rose from her safe position in the rocks and immediately burst into tears. I wrapped my arms around her and held her tight, and through my own tears, told her that Erik would be in the hospital in ten minutes.

We sat down amidst the boulders and snow and broke out some much needed food and water. Jessica told us what had happened hours earlier that morning.

She and Erik, both twenty-six, had hiked into the valley the evening before and set up camp. Erik had intended to ski the couloir the next morning, something he had done on a previous visit to the area. Jessica said that he had taken a camcorder and tripod along, with the intention of setting it up on the glacier below the couloir, in order to film his climb up, and subsequent ski descent.

She was not watching when he made his attempt. Unbeknownst to her, the two hikers had witnessed the fall and had hiked up the glacier to see if they could find Erik. When they located him in the crevasse, they yelled for help. Jessica heard their screams. She assumed that it may be Erik in trouble and started up the mountain herself. Another set of hikers moving along the trail in the valley below heard the screams and notified Leslie-the-Ranger near the north shore of the lake. Leslie hiked up the valley and made voice contact with the hikers, then called in the information.

From our vantage directly below the couloir, it was clear what had happened. Erik's climb up the couloir, skis strapped to his pack, was successful. Once he gained the top of the 700-foot-high chute, he removed his crampons and clipped into his skis. His turns were clearly visible in the snow for the first 200 feet, then, suddenly, the turn marks ended. It was obvious that at this point, Erik likely caught an edge, and he fell on the fifty-degree slope.

From his last ski track to the bottom of the chute, Erik made contact with the snow only once. He had virtually free-fallen for 500 feet and slammed directly into that giant boulder, then dropped into the crevasse. Even with a helmet, it was a miracle his head hadn't shattered from the impact.

We called down to our team members below and asked them to pack up Erik and Jessica's camp as the north face slipped into the afternoon shadows and temperatures sank. Once we gained the trail in the valley, we headed to the boat dock for the trip back across the lake.

By the time we reached the resort, Erik had been flown from the hospital in Mammoth Lakes, where he had been stabilized, to the trauma center at the renown Washoe Medical Center in Reno, Nevada.

After yet another first-class food fest with Carmen and Richard, we set off for home. I made my way to the airport in hopes of catching Jay and his crew before they headed back to their base in Fallon, but they had already lifted off. I pointed the truck toward home, all the while praying that Erik would survive his ordeal.

I shared the day's events with Leah and the two kids. We all prayed for Erik and Jessica. I called the base in Fallon and spoke to Jay, thanking him for their unfailing help.

"You know," he said, "I never did make contact with my base commander to get permission to fly the mission. You were so intent in the restaurant this morning that I decided to fly the mission anyway. I'm pretty sure my C.O.'ll be okay with it."

I wished him luck in explaining that to his commanding officer and told him I would keep him posted on Erik's condition.

Later that evening I called the medical center in Reno. They put me in touch with Jessica, who told me that Erik was still unconscious, but was breathing on his own. Amazingly, he had only fractured two fingers, and his head was unscathed. However, there was devastatingly bad news. Erik had sustained fractures of vertebrae in his neck and his back and likely had severe spinal cord damage. He also had a collapsed lung. I told Jessica that we would continue praying for his recovery and that I would talk to her the next day.

Erik regained consciousness two days after arriving at the trauma center. The fractured vertebrae in his back severed his spinal cord, and he was informed that he would be paralyzed from the chest down.

Erik stayed at the medical center for a couple of weeks and was then flown to a rehabilitation center in Colorado to begin the process of learning how to manage life as a paraplegic. Though I was heartbroken at the prospect of this young man's life being changed so radically, I was simply amazed that he was alive at all.

In the days that followed, I took stock of the myriad things that came together to produce such an extraordinary outcome on that day. It had all begun with a doctor's note that was carried out by a backpacker the night before. Had that doctor not been so thorough in providing the information he had, we may not have had the chopper there, which would have meant a longer response time for Erik's rescue and most certain death for him.

Had those hikers not witnessed Erik's fall; had Leslie not been close by with her radio; had I not been so insistent to Jay that we needed their help; had he waited to contact his C.O.; had Joe not been my partner that day; had CPR not worked, as it rarely does; had the helo not been able to hold the hover; had Joe not called for the alert to Care Flight. The list goes on and on and on.

Had even one of the many things that fell into place not occurred, Erik Schultz would have died that day on North Peak. So many things came together -- in the right place, and at just the right time.

Erik recovered from his injuries and, though wheelchair bound, returned to his job as director of the Arthur B. Schultz Foundation. He has become an advocate for wheelchair persons and has redirected the focus of his father's foundation to one that supports the needs of the mobility impaired.

I had the pure joy of filming Erik skiing in his "sit ski" on Mammoth Mountain a little more than a year after his accident. Erik and I reunited with the crew at Fallon Naval Air Station for a *People Magazine* photo shoot in the summer of 1999. Erik is an avid downhill and cross-country skier, kayaker, road biker, and is developing a chair with tracks that will allow him to ascend mountains.

Seeing Erik survive that horrific fall down North Peak, then go on to live a productive life that purposes to help the lives of others, makes me profoundly proud to call this man my friend. This is one of the true joys of being a search and rescue professional. Not only have I been blessed to use my skills to help others, I've been able to meet so many extraordinary people along the way. Thankfully, I've been fortunate to see far more rescues than recoveries.

Even now, as I think back on that extraordinary day, there is one scene that stands out vividly in my mind. It's a visual that reminds me so much of that iconic image captured by Joe Rosenthal on Mt. Suribachi -- a moment in time that transcends all others. Oh, what I would have given to have my own Joe Rosenthal on scene that day, recording the image of my partner, Joe Rousek, fighting for his own breath, and his first reaction to the tragedy before him was to call out to God in intercession for this perfect stranger. Between gasps from seared lungs, he managed to cry out only two words, "Lord! God!"

And God showed up.

CHAPTER 7

He gives strength to the weary,
and increases the power of the weak.

Isaiah 40:29

O ver the years I've come to the conclusion that the sport of
rock climbing really employs the skills of three different
sports or disciplines. First, climbing is very much like gymnastics,
requiring strength, flexibility and moments of sheer power.
Second, climbing is quite like ballet, where deftness of movement
and the ability to use the least amount of effort needed for any
given move saves precious energy. And last and most
importantly, climbing rocks is like the game of chess. One has to
give thought to the next move as well as consider the
consequences.

To be successful in the vertical world, one must have skills in
these areas, relying on one or all of them at a time, given the
situation. It is a matter of adjusting to the circumstance and then
choosing the path that will lead to success. Most of the time, these
decisions are made at a moments notice.

The ability to adapt to difficulties in the climbing realm is
what attracted me to the sport, and those characteristics carried
over into the world of Search and Rescue. Like the crises that
arise on a steep rock wall, so too "instant situations" arise when a
rescue call comes in, forcing one to adapt, focus, and most of all,
be flexible.

In the fall of 1998, Leah and I made the decision to build a new home. After completing the design work, I shelved all other projects in order to dedicate my time to the construction of our home. I would do most of the work myself and hoped to complete the house in a year. This would require me to work seven days a week and would take all my strength. It would have been easy to take a year off from SAR work, but my heart and soul said to keep myself available for any situation that might arise. I could only hope that the season would be a slow one.

With winter finally relenting in the spring of 1999, I managed to break ground, get a foundation in, and begin framing our dream house. It wasn't long before the phone started to ring with the rescues of summer.

On the 25th of June, the call came in for a missing eighty-two-year-old Alzheimer patient who had wandered away from his son's motor home at a local campground. For the next three days a team of nearly a hundred searchers, along with search dog and helicopter support, combed every stand of timber, waterway, meadow, rock hillside and canyon for what was initially thought would be an easy find.

Not only had no one else in the campground even seen the subject, we failed to find a single trace. One possible scenario was that the old gentleman had managed to get a ride and disappeared from the area entirely. We had certainly seen this with Alzheimer patients in the past. After three days and nights of frustrating results, the search was suspended.

I returned home exhausted from short nights and miles and miles of scratching through some of the thickest terrain I had ever encountered. And I was frustrated that we had been unsuccessful. My 4,200-foot-house-framing project was waiting for me.

Thankfully, the next two weeks passed without any rescue calls. My body had fully recovered just as I arrived at the meat of the framing on our home: a huge, steep and physically demanding roof line that was the crowning jewel of the house. I knew when I drew the plans that this portion of the construction would require me to be at my best, both mentally and physically.

Just as I was getting into the thick of things on that roof, the Sheriff came calling. I didn't know it at the time, but this one call would lead to a day of rescues that would take everything climbing had taught me about adapting and would push my abilities to the limit.

The call had a bit of optimism about it. On August 13th, some backpackers had wandered off the trail and gotten a bit lost. They reported finding what they described as "possible human remains" in a remote location. Where the optimism figured in was that the remains were found about a mile from where our missing Alzheimer patient had disappeared.

For the family of the missing, even finding the subject deceased offers a sense of closure and the ability to put the event behind them and move on. At least they aren't left wondering what became of their loved one. So we were optimistic that our search could bring them that closure.

I had been notified on a Friday afternoon, and the decision was made to assemble six team members to join the Sheriff/Coroner the following morning for the recovery detail.

I rose early that morning, stretching my aching body while trying to eat a good breakfast. The previous week of framing had left me in desperate need of rest. But the thought of being able to close a missing-person case energized me.

As I made the hour-long drive north to the trailhead, I steeled myself for the task at hand. Body recoveries are never pleasant, especially those that had been out in the wild for a few weeks. With all the wildlife out there, the scene could easily resemble something out of a Stephen King horror film. Based on the report taken from the backpackers and their description of "possible human remains," I had a pretty good idea what we were in for.

About twenty minutes into the drive, a call came over my mobile radio requesting a medic dispatch for a horseback rider who had broken her pelvis in a fall. I knew that the area where the victim was would be a good twenty- to thirty-minute hike for medic personnel and their gear. The local fire department had been dispatched, as well, to provide more manpower.

I was also aware that the rescue helicopter from the Navy base at Fallon was due to arrive at our local airport within the hour to provide training to some of our newest team members. Perhaps the helicopter could be contacted to provide assistance. I called the dispatcher on the radio and asked her to inform the Watch Commander.

Within a few minutes, the dispatcher called me back and said they had managed to reach the commanding officer at Fallon by phone. He had reached the chopper via cell phone; they were only twenty minutes away.

As I drew closer to the vicinity of the downed rider, I radioed the chopper and was able to guide them to the approximate location of the victim by giving them landmarks that I knew from memory. The medic crew had reached the injured woman by then and guided the helo to their exact location.

In a unique way I was able to assist in a rescue, though I was never at the scene and never closer than ten miles from the helicopter. I simply used one of the most valuable tools a SAR team member hopes to have: information. Once again, flexibility with circumstances created success. As I arrived at the designated meeting point for our "possible human remains" recovery detail, a lucky young woman was arriving at the hospital in the capable hands of the Navy.

With no time lost from that incident, we started our detail at 7:00 a.m. I was met at the trailhead by five other team members and Lt. Steve Maris, our County Coroner. We hiked to the site armed with rubber gloves, a body bag, and a wheeled litter to transport the remains.

About half a mile from where our missing subject had disappeared from the motor home two weeks earlier, we left the trail, crossed a roaring creek, and began ascending a steep hillside. Within a few minutes of leaving the trail, I had the thought that the remains we were going after might quite possibly be those of another subject. Though it was early and quite cool, we were working up a sweat. This terrain was far too difficult for an eighty-two year old in failing health.

After about twenty minutes of thick brush and trees, the area opened into a thin forest. The hiking got a bit easier and the steepness relented. The backpackers who had reported the find had said to look for a prominent rock outcrop that marked the vicinity of the remains. As we approached that spot, the cool morning air pushing down from the high country above brought with it the familiar scent of death. Someone or *something* had died here.

The first bit of remains proved to be, indeed, human: a fully intact pelvis with a bit of tissue. Not far away lay a femur, clearly gnawed clean by large teeth and, just beyond that, a fully intact and mummified left hand.

The search area spread out as our sense of smell drew us deeper into the surrounding landscape. It was clear that making an identification was going to be a challenge, as the body had been ripped to shreds. We really needed to find the skull for dental-record assistance.

A few minutes later we made a crucial find: an entire spinal column. Hopefully, the skull would not be far away. I searched about thirty yards uphill of what seemed to be the main area of remains. It was here that I found the contents of a wallet. All of the items had the name of our missing subject. It wasn't as conclusive as the skull, but it was evidence that would help.

Not long afterward, another team member found the second femur, along with clothing that matched the description given by the son two weeks prior. It seemed conclusive that we had found our missing subject, but only the skull or a DNA test on the existing remains would prove that beyond all doubt. We continued our search in an ever-widening grid pattern.

After three hours of searching, the lieutenant said enough was enough. As we were bagging all of the remains for the hike out, someone spotted a small piece of evidence lying among the pine needles very near where the majority of the bones were collected.

It was the small, silver medical alert bracelet our missing man had been wearing, identifying him as an Alzheimer patient.

We packaged the remains and headed back down the hill, all the while mulling over the possible scenarios that would have allowed an eighty-two-year-old man up such a steep location.

We finally concluded that somehow the old gentleman had managed to walk over half a mile through a crowded campground without anyone seeing or noticing him. Then, in all likelihood, he had drowned while attempting to cross the creek. Somehow the body had been missed, even though the area had been repeatedly searched by both personnel and dog teams.

After he had drowned, a bear or mountain lion pulled the body from the water and dragged it up the slope to that quiet spot in the forest and had had a feast. What the bear or cat didn't eat, the rest of the forest's creatures scattered out over the hillside.

Based on the remains we collected, as well as other physical evidence, the Coroner issued a death certificate in the name of our missing man. A few weeks later one of our team members who handles a search dog, used the area for training, along with two other dog teams. During their exercise, the dogs located the missing skull nearly 200 yards downhill of the main area of remains.

In spite of the morning's gruesome task, all of us were powerfully hungry for lunch. It was just after noon when we headed into Bridgeport and walked into a Mexican restaurant for refueling.

No sooner had we ordered than the beeping of our pagers filled the room, hailing us to the third incident of the day. Two high-school boys on a training run with their cross-country team had taken a wrong trail and were missing. The incident was an hour's drive away. There were plenty of other team members in the Mammoth Lakes area for the helicopter training that morning who would respond, so we elected to take the time to eat before heading that way.

Not two minutes after our pagers went off, my cell phone

rang. It was the Watch Commander. A call had just come in from a hiker at a nearby trailhead reporting a woman backpacker very ill with symptoms of what sounded like acute mountain sickness (AMS) or altitude sickness.

AMS is a fairly common cause of summertime rescues. The root of the illness tends to be dehydration and gaining elevation too quickly. Though AMS is not usually fatal, it can lead to edema in either the lungs or the brain as the body tries to adjust to oxygen-starvation from exertion or dehydration at altitude. Both pulmonary and cerebral edema can be fatal.

The three best cures for AMS are lots of clear fluids, oxygen, and a descent in altitude. This is where most folks usually get in trouble. Getting a person to a lower elevation can be a daunting task, especially when that subject is too ill to move.

Our sick backpacker was five and a half miles into the backcountry from the trailhead. I relayed the information to the lieutenant and my other teammates, and we formulated our plan. The trailhead was a ten-mile drive from our location, mostly on dirt roads. The rest of the team was responding to the missing boys and were an hour away. We would handle this one on our own.

The plan was for me to race in to the trailhead then speed-hike to the victim. Two other team members would wait for the medic unit at the trailhead and follow in behind me with oxygen bottles. I grabbed my two fish tacos-to-go and headed for the door.

As I drove, I radioed dispatch and asked them to find out the status of the Navy helo. The training that morning would have only lasted until noon. In all likelihood the crew would eat lunch with the team in Mammoth then head back to Fallon. If they were available, and if the victim was as ill as reported, we were going to need that helicopter.

Eating fish tacos in a restaurant is normally a multiple napkin ordeal. But doing it while bouncing down a dirt road, trying to drive *and* talking on the radio, is downright comical. It wasn't long before I gave up on being neat.

With all the energy spent during the morning recovery mission, I was famished. And with what I was about to do, I needed every bit of nourishment I could get in me. I had plenty of food in my pack, but no time to eat anything once I reached the trailhead. What had been two very appetizing tacos when I left the restaurant were now a jumbled mass of ingredients scattered on my lap. I stuffed the entire mess in my mouth and licked my fingers clean.

The dispatcher got back to me and said that the helo crew had just reached their base, were refueling, and would lift off and head my way in a matter of minutes. Their flight time to reach the backpacker at Nutter Lake was just under an hour. It was an uphill hike of five miles for me. I would have to set some sort of record to reach the victim before the chopper arrived. As soon as I arrived at the trailhead, I pulled on my pack and headed in full steam.

Our subject that day was a sixty-two-year-old woman who had been on trail for three days and sick for the past two. At the time of the report she was too dizzy to stand, had extreme nausea, and was refusing liquids. It was clear she was very ill. My goal was to reach her ahead of the helo and assess her condition, administer whatever first-aid possible, and then locate a good landing zone (LZ) for the chopper.

At the halfway point I received a radio call from my two teammates informing me they were at the trailhead with the O2. I told them it was likely that the helo would arrive with oxygen long before they could get to the scene, but to go ahead and start in behind me in case the chopper was unable to make it. This was standard procedure, as over the years we have seen air service get turned back for myriad reasons.

I was doing what I call Level-Four hiking. On my scale, Level One is walking, and Level Five is a full run. The afternoon sun was hot and I was drenched in sweat. As I crossed a small creek at about the three-and-a-half-mile mark, I stopped for a moment, filled my hat with water, and dumped it over my head. I had been on the trail for thirty-five minutes.

At mile four, the trail ascended a north-facing slope and was considerably cooler in the afternoon shade. I picked up the pace and pushed hard up the hill. At its top, the trail was flat with a few downhill sections, so I went to Level Five.

As I reached the north end of Nutter Lake, I asked a hiker if he knew the whereabouts of the sick woman. He told me I would find her at the southeast end of the lake. I thanked him and ran on. A few minutes later, I came upon the subject and the rest of her party. I radioed to my teammates and let them know I was on scene then checked my watch. The five-plus-mile hike had taken me fifty-eight minutes.

I got the woman to sit up and insisted she drink the quart of water I handed her. She vomited most of it. Clearly she needed oxygen and a helicopter ride.

The area we were in had no LZ whatsoever, and, based on her condition, I knew I needed help getting her to another spot. Then I heard it – the familiar thump-thump of the helicopter echoing up the canyon. The woman perked up when I told her that it was for her.

As the helo drew close, I made radio contact and set off a smoke bomb to show our location. I informed the crew they would have to find an LZ from the air, and in all likelihood, we would need to get her on O2 before moving her. Within a few minutes, the chopper set down about 250 yards away, and two crewmen brought oxygen to our location.

After only five minutes of pure oxygen, the woman was able to get on her feet and allowed us to assist her to the chopper. Both she and I got aboard with our packs. We were off, grateful that we didn't have to walk out of there. I radioed my teammates and let them know they could return to the trailhead.

Ten minutes later, we landed at the hospital in Bridgeport and turned our grateful patient over to the hospital staff. Between the oxygen and lower elevation, she was recovering. I said my goodbyes to the helicopter crew and thanked them for their second trip of the day to our operations.

Sgt. Turner came by and picked me up then drove me back to the trailhead to get my truck.

"The boys were found pretty quickly," he said. "How 'bout I buy you some dinner."

"Thank you, Sir, but I think I'll call Leah and have dinner with the family."

"You know," he said, "we matched a record today. Four operations in one twenty-four-hour period."

I looked at my watch. It was only about 5:30 p.m.

"Yah, but the day is still young," I reminded him, with a tired smile on my face.

As I headed back down the highway to meet my family, my thoughts traveled from going over the events of the day to the work that awaited me back at home. I had planned on being home early that afternoon, once the body recovery was done, so that I could get a few more things done on the house. But I had no regrets. I felt I had done what I was supposed to do, and I was content with our success.

I pulled into the parking lot of a restaurant in Lee Vining and was about to get out of my truck when my cell phone rang.

"Would you believe number five?"

It was Sgt. Turner, and he was as incredulous as I was.

"We have a subject with a possible broken femur at Robinson Lake," he said. "I need you to get back to Bridgeport, get on the helo, and try to get in there before dark! I've already notified the chopper and they're in flight to the airfield here in Bridgeport to pick you up."

I'm on my way!"

As I exited the parking lot, Leah and the kids pulled in. I gave her the quick details, and she was *not* pleased.

"I don't think I'll make it home tonight. I'm so sorry. But you guys go ahead and enjoy dinner. I'll see you tomorrow after church.

"Oh! And pray for me," I yelled, as I headed out onto the highway and steered my truck north.

As I raced back through Lee Vining, I spotted the two teammates who had been with me on the last operation, heading back south. I got on the radio.

"Guys, we have another event, and we could really use your help."

"Copy that, Dean. We're with you."

"Okay, I'll need one of you to go in with me, and the other at the base working communications."

"Roger that."

They turned around and fell in behind me. I called dispatch for additional information. I was told a forty-five-year-old man who was camped at Robinson Lake with his family had taken a fall among some boulders while fishing. He may have broken his femur. They managed to get him back to his tent, but he was in tremendous pain.

The femur is the largest bone in the body, and when it breaks the pain is massive, on a scale with childbirth. Every movement is torture, and the risk of internal bleeding is life threatening.

Robinson Lake is a stiff eight-mile hike from the trailhead where we had started our day for the recovery mission. We raced north to meet the helo, and I kept my eyes on the sun as it neared the top of the Sierra crest. I was skeptical about our chances of having enough daylight to make the flight in there. It was going to be close.

As I drove, my thoughts turned back to food. I had been on the go all day and had taken in limited calories in comparison to what I had been burning. Clearly, this mission was time sensitive and the chances of getting much to eat prior to boarding the chopper would be slim. The jail kitchen was just a stone's throw from the airfield. I called the Watch Commander.

"Hey Sarge, can you do me a favor? Can you meet us at the airport with a plate of food from the jail kitchen? That dash up to Nutter Lake drained my tank."

"Oh, and Bill and Victor are with me. They're needing calories, too!"

"I'll take care of it!" he said.

I turned my attention back to planning the mission. The two team members following me would be perfect for the task. Bill Green had a full pack and was completely ready to head in for the night. Though his backcountry experience was somewhat limited, he was in decent enough shape to handle the terrain, was an expert on radio communications, GPS and map reading, and was highly motivated.

Victor Aguirre was the perfect man to run our operations base: an expert on the radio as well and detail oriented. He also had enough mission experience to know what we would be going through in the field and why we would request certain things. With the compliment of the Navy crew on the helo, we had a strong team.

When we reached the airfield, we were met by the Watch Commander and, true to his word, he had three plates of food for us. We dined that evening off the truck tailgate while doing an equipment check. The chopper was just a few minutes out.

I knew the crew must be feeling the hours of the day as we were. They had lifted off that morning at 6:30 with the intent of coming to our neck of the woods for a simple training day, only to be involved in two rescues as well. Now, twelve hours later, they were asked to fly the most difficult mission of the day. My experience with these men and women told me they were completely up to the task.

The one thing we didn't have going for us was time. Within minutes, the sun would be behind the crest of the ridge, throwing the canyon we needed to fly up into deep shadow. We knew there would not be time for a briefing of the crew for this mission. As the chopper approached the field, we radioed them a coordinate for the lake so they could plug it into their on-board GPS guidance system.

"Do you think we need to call in additional personnel?" The

Watch Commander, Sgt. Turner, asked me.

"That probably won't be necessary," I said. "Bill and Victor and I should be able to handle this."

"Yah, and it'll be dark soon. There isn't really time to fly more team in," Sgt. Turner mused.

We planned to spend the night with the victim, stabilizing him, then fly him out at first light. Even if the chopper were not available in the morning, the thought of wheeling the subject down eight miles and nearly 4,000 vertical feet of trail was out of the question. We would simply have to wait for an available chopper ride.

We were confident that additional personnel would be a waste of resources, and the way the day had been going so far, the rest of the team may be needed elsewhere.

That familiar thump-thump sounded again, and the chopper set down just long enough for Bill and me to load our gear and climb aboard. I put on a flight helmet so I could speak with our pilot, Lt. Dave Cotts.

"It'll be getting dark pretty soon," he said. "What do you know about potential landing zones at the lake?"

The rotors roared above us. "Our victim was reported to be near the east shore," I said into the mic, "but there's a small clearing just north of the lake on a knoll."

"Roger that."

In just a few minutes, we turned into the canyon, and, as expected, the area was already in full shadow. As the canyon bends to the south, it is capped by a stunning 11,346 foot-high rocky peak known as Crown Point. Robinson Lake lies at the peak's northern base, at just over 10,000 feet. As Crown Point came into view, it became clear we were too late. The light was too far gone. It was time for some quick decision making.

We were directly over Barney Lake, which was at the halfway point between the trailhead and the victim's location.

"LT, can you get us down to the lake? We can hike in from there."

"Will do."

With all the lights on, we descended in a spiral, headed for the south shore of the lake, which had the fewest trees.

"Lieutenant, I'd like to take Corpsman Vandercook with us to help assess the victim's injury."

"I can do that," said Cooky, "but I don't have the gear to be out all night."

"We're carrying enough gear for the three of us," I assured him.

He gathered up his medical equipment and readied to go with us.

As we approached our intended landing zone, we suddenly noticed two tents pitched at the site. We simply could not see them in the fading light while at higher altitude.

"There's a clear area of beach between the tents and the lake," I pointed out.

"That beach might be too soft for a landing," he said.

Light was nearly gone now and we had no more time.

"Hover low over the beach," I said. "We'll throw out our gear and jump."

"I can do the low hover, but the rotor wash will likely blow over the tents in the camp."

"We got a guy with a broken femur down there. A few leveled tents is a low price to pay to get to him."

Lt. Cotts swung the helo out over the lake and came in for our final approach. The startled backpackers beat a hasty retreat from the blast of the rotor blades. We threw open the side door, pitched out our gear, and jumped.

I signaled a thumbs-up to the crew and, within seconds, they were up and on their way to the airport to wait out the night.

We gathered up our gear and walked over to the bewildered backpackers. After assuring them we were not the Marines coming to take over their camp, we filled them in on the situation, made apologies for destroying their campsite, bid them goodnight and headed up the trail.

We were now faced with the latter half of the eight-mile hike to the lake. Unfortunately, this second four-mile stretch was the steeper section, with over 2,000 feet of elevation gain. The warm temperatures of daytime were rapidly cooling.

Cooky proved a willing party to the suffering. We all carried heavy loads, but he did not have the advantage of living at altitude like Bill and I, and clearly he was not used to this kind of physical abuse. We tried keeping him involved in conversation to take his mind off the strains of the trail, but his deep gasps made words too much to manage. We plodded up the switch-backed trail, following the light of our headlamps.

After an hour and a half, we reached the top and a junction in the trail. As the wind picked up, the temperature plummeted. We stopped for a break and pulled out additional clothing. With no signage at the trail junction, we broke out the map and took a GPS reading. I was certain the lake was to the east, but it had been ten years since my last visit to this particular area. We took the trail headed east. It was 8:30 p.m.

Twenty minutes later, we reached the west shore of Robinson Lake. We called out in the darkness, hoping to hear a response. Finally, a voice called back. Minutes later, a man approached us in the darkness. He was the leader of a group of young people camped above the north shore. He was aware of the injured man and directed us to a faint fishermen's trail that traversed the southwest side of the lake and would take us to the victim. We thanked him and made our way around the lake, arriving at the camp at 11:30. The hike had taken us two and a half hours.

The victim was lying in his tent, surrounded by his wife and two kids. He had been resting comfortably, but any movement was excruciating. Cooky assessed the man's injuries. Clearly he had sustained pretty serious trauma to his upper leg, but Cooky was confident the leg was not broken. We splinted the leg and told everyone we would evacuate him via helicopter at dawn.

Another couple camped with the family went to work upon our arrival. They had lit a fire and were cooking a warm meal for us, which we appreciated and consumed in short order. They informed us that they had used llamas to haul in their gear, which explained the strange sounds coming from a nearby stand of trees.

Bill and I needed to communicate with Victor at SAR base to let him know our status and to brief the chopper crew for the morning plans. From our position at the lake, we were unable to make radio contact, so I scrambled up to the top of a nearby rock outcrop. I had brought along a five-foot-long extendable antenna for my radio and used it to reach Victor. With the chopper crew briefed, everything was set for the morning.

Though the warm fire was inviting, all three of us were desperate for sleep. We said our goodnights and headed for our sleeping bags. I pulled out my bag and handed it to Cooky who was delighted to take it. The temperature had dipped below freezing and all he had were the clothes on his back. He slid into the bag and within minutes, was snoring.

Bill and I laid our insulated pads side by side. I got into my warmest clothes, and slipped into my bivy sack, a waterproof liner normally used with a sleeping bag when bivouacking without a tent. Bill unzipped his bag and threw it over both of us. We spent the next three hours listening to Cooky snore.

Bill and I climbed out of our frost-covered position at 5:30 a.m. The sky was hinting at another spectacular day. I had to threaten Cooky with a dousing in the lake to get him to exit the warm confines of my dearly missed sleeping bag.

Our hosts built a warm fire and set about preparing a fine breakfast for us all. Cooky assisted our injured man and got him ready to move. Bill headed up to the rock outcrop to make radio contact, while I scouted a good landing zone. Our subject was clearly not keen on movement.

About a hundred yards from camp, a small peninsula extended out into the lake and away from the tree-lined shore. As long as it didn't have any wind to deal with, the chopper could approach from right over the water, hover over the peninsula and winch the man into the helo. I briefed Cooky on the plan and he agreed it looked like the best option.

We finished breakfast and packed our gear. Bill radioed Victor and let him know we were heading for the landing zone and should be in place in thirty minutes. Carefully, we assisted our patient over rocks and around trees to the little rock island.

The chopper appeared and circled our position. We radioed them our plan and they agreed to it. The crew dropped a pack containing harnesses for both Cooky and the victim. We got our patient into a full-body harness so as not to put undo pressure on his leg. The chopper entered a hover twenty feet above us and lowered the winch cable. With Cooky and the patient connected, I gave a thumbs-up, and they were winched aboard. Ten minutes later they set down at the hospital in Bridgeport.

Bill and I said our goodbyes to the man's family and the other campers. Within a few minutes the chopper returned, did a one-skid landing on the rock peninsula, and we climbed aboard. What a pleasure it was to forgo the eight-mile hike out for a quick chopper ride. Within minutes we were back in Bridgeport enjoying a meal with the chopper crew and the Sheriff.

After our debriefing session, I eased my weary body behind the wheel of my truck and pointed it towards home. As I drove, I considered turning off the radio, pager, and my cell phone. My thoughts bounced back and forth between the work waiting for me at home, and the events of the past day.

Over the last thirty hours I had been involved, in one way or another, in five operations, a new county record. The statistics were exhausting. In those thirty hours, I had personally driven 242 miles, hiked twelve and a half miles gaining almost 5,000 feet of elevation while carrying nearly fifty pounds in my pack, and logged over forty miles in the helicopter.

My efforts and those of my teammates had saved three lives, along with recovering the remains of a loved one for a family who would now be able to move on with their lives. I was grateful for the opportunity to serve these people and work alongside like-minded professionals.

Together, we had adapted to whatever came along and had risen to the challenge. And though my body was wracked with fatigue and exhaustion, God had sustained me through those challenges to help us all to a positive outcome.

Fifteen miles from home my phone rang. I hesitated for a few seconds when the caller I.D. showed that it is was the number for the Sheriff's office. I answered warily.

"What now?"

"Lieutenant Hampton here. You won't believe this, but . . . Hah! I'm just pullin' your leg! Go home. You're late for work!"

CHAPTER 8

A friend loves at all times,
and a brother is born for adversity.

Proverbs 17:17

I am convinced that God has gifted each of us with certain passions that make us tick. I also believe that no matter what our passion might be, we can use it to benefit others. Theologian and author Frederick Buechner once wrote, "*The place where God calls you is the place where your deep gladness, and the world's great hunger, meet.*"

I realized early in life that spending my years as a SAR professional was not only a worthy cause, it simply filled a longing in my heart to help others in a unique way. It allowed me to be out in the high and wild places that I love and to use my skills to make a difference in someone else's life. It's been what I refer to as "peas and carrots" -- one of those things you just know is right for you, in every way. It's my milieu; it suits me.

Though I've recovered sixty-six bodies over the course of my career, the positive outcomes have far outweighed the deaths. It has been a blessing to know that, along with the help of myriad like-minded professional teammates, I have saved lives.

Like the bonds I've created with climbing partners over the years, some of these SAR team friendships have changed my life in profound ways. Most of them were forged in the fires of adversity. My bond with Pete was only one of many.

I remember liking Chuck Bauss from the first time I saw him at one of our SAR team meetings. He was a volunteer fireman in Mammoth Lakes and was interested in getting involved in SAR as well. He came to us with virtually no backcountry skills or experience. What he lacked in ability, he made up for with a strong desire to learn. Not long after I met him, he said to me, "I want to know what you know." Chuck had a teachable heart -- something I simply loved about the guy.

One particularly cold and snowy evening, the team was called out to find a missing snowboarder on Mammoth Mountain. The subject, Tom Miller, had been riding with friends all afternoon in a heavy snowfall and disappeared. Mammoth Ski Patrol was unable to find him before darkness fell.

As I made my way to our search base at the ski area Main Lodge, Chuck called me on my cell phone and told me that he had family commitments and would be unable to make it. I could hear the disappointment in his voice, but I assured him there would be plenty more opportunities in the future. His home was just off the ski area, so he told me he would monitor our search with his radio. He wished us good luck.

My teammates and I were to search for Tom Miller, armed with information his friends had given us regarding the point he was last seen. It was now well after dark, although a full moon rose high in the sky. The storm had cleared, and the temperature had plummeted to near zero. We made our way to a steep area on the mountain with lots of rocky outcroppings.

About an hour after we began our descent and search, one of my teammates came across Tom. He had obviously sustained serious trauma after taking a huge fall into the rocks. He had lain prone for over four hours in brutally cold conditions. He was barely alive.

We quickly packaged Tom into a sled litter and descended to the lodge and a waiting ambulance. At his home just a few blocks away, Chuck was following every word of our radio traffic. He knew the difficulties we had faced in the bitterly cold conditions. I thought of him often that night, knowing how dedicated he was to the team and how badly he wanted to be out there with us.

After ten minutes of skiing, we arrived at the lodge. Waiting there at the ambulance, along with Tom's friends, was Chuck. We looked at each other. His eyes told me how much he had wanted to help up there, and mine told him how grave Tom's condition was. Chuck pitched in helping the medics immediately, getting Tom onto a gurney and into the back of the ambulance.

After shedding my skis and pack, I went over and talked with Tom's friends to give them as much information as I could. They told me about his wife and child and what a great friend he was to all of them. I was very clear with them that he was not in good shape. Together, we prayed for his survival. I gave them directions to the hospital and told them I would see them there.

As I gathered my gear, I walked past the back of the ambulance. Climbing up on the bumper, I scraped the ice off the back window and peered in. There, between the two medics and a menagerie of I.V. lines, was Chuck, hard at work performing CPR on Tom. My heart swelled with pride for my friend. He stayed with us in spirit while we were on the mountain then showed up to help fight for a life.

We moved on down to the trauma room at Mammoth Hospital and spent the next five hours working with the ER staff, fighting for Tom's life. Through it all, Chuck never stopped taking his turn at performing CPR. Though the world lost Tom Miller that awful night, an extraordinary young man fought for him to the very end.

Over the years, Chuck was a willing student, drinking in everything I had to teach him. Together, we spent extraordinary days saving lives. On July 28, 1999, Chuck and I shared a SAR experience that would introduce the two of us to the most amazing patient I have ever encountered in all my years of rescue work.

That summer, I had hired Chuck to help me build our new home. We had been working hard joisting a floor that day. Not long after lunch my phone rang. A hiker was injured high on the south face of North Peak.

Chuck and I jumped into my truck and raced to Tioga Pass. This would be Chuck's first rescue operation on North Peak and my seventh. I had climbed the peak many times on my own, so I knew it intimately.

We arrived at the marina at Saddlebag Lake. Once again, Richard Ernst and his boat were ready and waiting for us. We threw our gear aboard and headed across the lake. One of Richard's staff was along for the ride and filled us in on the information they had.

A hiker had taken a sliding fall on the south face of the peak and was complaining of hip pain and unable to walk. I knew that side of the peak well; it was my normal descent route. It consisted of a fifty-degree slope of loose rock and decomposing granite -- certainly an easy place to lose one's footing.

Once on the north shore, we made a mad dash up the peak, carrying a rescue litter between us. I had already requested the Navy chopper, so we were intent on getting on-scene prior to the arrival of the helo. We alternated between Level-Four and Five hiking, really pushing ourselves.

Chuck and I arrived on the scene around 5:30 p.m. Our injured subject, Peter Berrington, was calmly lying on his back, completely relaxed. Sitting alongside him were his daughter, Stephanie, and son-in-law, Tom, along with Courtney, a family friend.

I asked Peter basic questions to assess his mental status: his name, where he was from, did he know where he was, etc. He answered me with a very proper British accent. Making notes, I asked, "Peter, what are you, about sixty-five or so?"

Peter was clearly fit. He smiled a broad smile, and with a twinkle in his eyes, replied, "I'm eighty." Chuck and I were dumbfounded.

Very matter-of-factly, Peter told us about their attempt to reach the summit, and how they had turned back just above where he had fallen at the 11,600 foot level. He didn't remember what caused his fall -- he simply began to slide. He went about forty feet before coming to a stop.

Examining him, Chuck and I determined that he had a possible fractured pelvis, a very painful injury. Cautiously, we loaded Peter into the litter and made him warm and comfortable. He never complained one bit. Honestly, he never even winced.

We explained how things would go once the chopper arrived and assured Peter he would be in the hospital in Mammoth very soon. While waiting, Peter regaled us with tales of his life as a Constable in India, during the British Raj. Chuck and I were mesmerized by this man and the life he had lived. And now, here he was at nearly 12,000 feet on the side of a peak in the high Sierra with a likely busted hip and not a single complaint.

At 6:30 p.m., we heard the first sound of the approaching chopper. In all my years of SAR, this was the first time I was disappointed that the helo was here. I was *so* fascinated with this man, I didn't want the conversation to end.

I popped a smoke bomb and the crew brought the chopper into a hover over us, lowered their winch cable, and hauled Peter into the bird. With Peter taken care of, we made our way off the peak with Tom, Stephanie and Courtney and headed home. Chuck stopped in at the hospital in Mammoth later that evening with his family to say "hi," a gesture Peter appreciated.

Peter recovered quickly after his surgery for a broken hip, and he and I corresponded on a regular basis. Of his experience that day on North Peak, he wrote, "Despite the inconvenience, it was an exciting, exhilarating experience, and I enjoyed it."

Leah and I had the pleasure of hosting Peter and his family as dinner guests in our home, and we spent time with them at their Mammoth vacation home as well. I was privileged to have dinner with Peter and his family at their Malibu home in 2014. The perfect gentleman, Peter was dressed in coat and tie and shared amazing stories all evening.

In February of 2015, Peter took a fall on his driveway, and on

March 13th, he passed away from complications. He was ninety-six years young. I was humbled beyond belief when his family asked me to deliver the eulogy at his memorial service.

Chuck and I still marvel at this amazing man, someone we would never have had the privilege to meet had we not been volunteers with the SAR team. Peter's humble nature and complete trust in us made our jobs infinitely easier, and his life continues to inspire our own. Peter requested that, upon his death, donations made in his memory be made to the SAR team. I've dealt with hundreds of patients over the years, but I am quite certain I will never forget Peter Berrington. A true gentleman -- and truly a gentle man.

Though the world of SAR can be dramatic, there have been plenty of hilarious events, as well. At times, I've used comedy to help lighten the stress.

I'm a "burn the candle at both ends" kinda' guy. I'm up every morning no later than 3:30, I get lots done during the day and go down hard no later than 10:00 p.m.

The summer months are always the busiest, and we were experiencing a rapid succession of SAR calls -- seems the Sheriff had me on speed dial. And, true to form, most SAR calls come at the worst hours of the night -- for most people. During this particular time, I was getting called in the wee hours of the morning, when normal people saw logs.

It had been literally three nights in a row of calls, well after midnight. When the fourth call came in at zero dark thirty, I was in a dead sleep. I saw that it was the Sheriff and answered, "Hurt . . . sick . . . lost . . . or dead?"

The watch commander busted out laughing, and said, "Rosnau, you are a piece of work."

After days away on missions, I found myself home one late afternoon and ready for a shower. While I was shaving, the Sheriff came calling with a time-sensitive mission. I dashed out the door.

An hour later, I met my teammates at a trailhead in the dark, and we began a 13-mile hike into the victim. After locating and stabilizing the subject, we waited out the night until first light when a chopper came in to extricate the man. Once the sun was high enough to forgo headlamps, one of my teammates said, "So, Rosnau . . . is that some sort of new look?"

I became the brunt of lots of laughter and joking, not having a clue what was so funny. But the guys were all looking at my face strangely. I reached my hand up to my face and felt stubble on one side of it and smooth skin on the other. Then I laughed as it dawned on me. I had run out of the house after shaving only one side of my face. Dropping everything and going at a moment's notice was Pete's way. He taught me well.

Over the years, I've dealt with various types of wounds that victims have suffered in the backcountry. From splinting broken bones to recovering brain matter, I've seen the human body pay dearly in the mountains.

Dealing with wounds to the head can be traumatic, as the smallest puncture elicits an absolute geyser of blood. Staunching that flow can prove challenging, especially with a patient going into shock, knowing they are many miles from a hospital.

I discovered early that the best dressing for head wounds are feminine maxi pads and tampons, so I regularly carried these in my pack. Often, these victims were flown out, arriving at the hospital long before I made it out of the backcountry. I developed a reputation with my bandage choice, so much so that when the victim arrived in the emergency room with maxi pads duct taped to their head and tampons stuffed up their nose, the staff would chuckle and say to the victim, "We see you've met Dean."

One event that will forever stick in my mind occurred in the winter of 1997. We were called out on a very snowy night to search for a snowmobiler who had become separated from the group and was in whiteout conditions just north of Mammoth

Lakes.

We needed to use the Sheriff's Department snow cat to pack down a trail for our search team snowmobiles in the deepening powder. We assembled at a designated meeting area along the highway and unloaded the snow cat from the trailer. The cat would be operated that night by Sgt. Boe Turner.

Sgt. Turner was in charge of the County Office of Emergency Services, and I had worked alongside him on many rescues over the years. In all ways, he was a likable and capable guy.

On this particular night, I was surprised when I saw that Boe had arrived at SAR base wearing only jeans and a short-sleeved shirt. As we boarded the snow cat, I told him I was concerned about his lack of winter clothing. I reminded him that things happen. Snow cats break down, and he may need to get out of the machine at some point.

Boe told us that when the call came in for the search, he had been at a dinner party, and he didn't want to take the time to go home for a change of clothes. He also mentioned that he had consumed a large quantity of Mexican food, and his stomach was feeling a bit queasy. The ride in the snow cat is not the smoothest thing in the world, and Boe moaned at every bump.

Outside in the darkness, the storm raged. The snowfall increased, and the howling wind whipped it into a frenzy. After an hour of pounding in the snow cat, Boe's bowels were raging as well. Sweat poured from his forehead, and he winced at every bump. After ninety minutes of pain and agony, Boe couldn't take it anymore; he needed to stop and take care of business.

Unfortunately, Boe's light attire was hardly ideal for jumping into four feet of fresh, icy powder, with temperatures in the teens. But circumstances had grown beyond his control. He brought the snow cat to a halt and exited the cab in haste. My partners and I followed. This was just too good to miss.

As he stepped off the cat track, he disappeared up to his crotch. Clearly, he was in dire pain and did not even take the time to find a tree for privacy. Boe stomped out a flat spot in the snow and un-hitched his drawers with his ungloved and rapidly freezing hands. In seconds, his jeans and skivvies were around his ankles, and he assumed the position while I gleefully yelled out, "Fire in the hole!"

Up to this point, we had all found this whole scene completely hilarious, as we reveled in making Boe feel even worse with our jabs and taunting. Unfortunately for all of us, Boe's aim was not true.

In his haste, he had emptied the entire contents of his wretched bowel right into the heart of his jeans and skivvies. Boe cursed his predicament at the top of his lungs, drowning out the howl of the wind, while the rest of us nearly herniated ourselves from laughter! Needless to say, none of us offered any measure of assistance.

Half frozen and getting colder by the second, Boe reluctantly pulled the offensive clothing back into position around his frostbitten man bits and climbed back into the snow cat. Fortunately for my partner and me, we were very near our drop off point, as the stench now fouling the snow cat was simply unbearable. At the appointed spot, we bailed out of the cab as if it were on fire.

I never thought that snowshoeing in the dark in deep powder in a whiteout in sub-freezing temperatures and having to navigate by GPS could feel so good. *Anything* was better than being in that cab.

After a few hours of searching a canyon we suspected he might have gone down, my partner and I came across the missing snowmobiler, cold, hungry, and thirsty, but otherwise alright. His machine was hopelessly stuck, so we hiked him down the canyon to a rendezvous point with Boe and his putrid snow cat.

Within seconds of boarding, our subject was willing to go back to his snowmobile and take his chances in the storm. The snow cat's heater had turned the cab into a cesspool of odor. The ninety-minute ride back to our search base was brutal.

In the grand scheme of things, this was a textbook SAR

mission. With the information provided to us and our knowledge of the area, we found the victim (he was incredulous that we would be out looking for him in that storm) and he lived to tell the tale.

All of us who had the misfortune of riding with Boe in the cat went home with a strong aversion to Mexican food. Boe went home to launder himself and burn his clothing. And I went home with two photos of Boe that I now consider priceless.

Webster's defines the term *gallows humor* as the following:

Any humor that treats serious matters such as death, war, disease, and crime, in a light, silly or satirical fashion.

To the lay person, this type of humor may seem incredibly insensitive. But for those who deal with intense and often disturbing scenes, gallows humor is a necessity. Without it, the stress becomes unbearable. Pete Schoerner introduced me to its value. He was a master at it, and it was my pleasure to carry on the tradition.

A light plane had gone down in the high country in winter, killing both occupants and trapping their bodies in the aircraft. We reached the crash site with Coroner Lt. Steve Maris and set about cutting the victims from the wreckage. The pilot, a man, was fairly easy to remove. However, the woman in the co-pilot's seat was a different story.

She was pinned tightly in the wreckage and had frozen to the seat. Her body had also suffered a tremendous amount of damage, particularly to the face and skull, rendering the scene horrifying. Even Maris, who dealt with bodies all the time, was stunned by the sight.

We had tried to extricate her for quite awhile and were losing daylight. In desperation, I crawled into the remains of the fuselage, and squeezed myself behind the seat. I then had Maris pull on the seat from the front, as I pushed with my legs. Suddenly the seat broke free and flew forward, sending Maris onto his back. The body landed on top of him, literally face to face.

Without missing a beat, I leaned over the body and looked at Maris.

"You two need a little alone time?"

His response will not be printed here, but I can unequivocally say that it was colorful. Only after that body was in the bag, still attached to the plane's seat, was Maris able to enjoy my humor.

Of course, we only used this kind of sardonic humor among ourselves and only when we needed to take the edge off. Though recovering bodies is an unpleasant task, we always considered what we were doing to be a great service to the family of the deceased.

After each SAR event, we spent time debriefing. Going over what had gone wrong and what had gone right always proved a valuable exercise. And in those times together, we grew stronger as a team.

Working with so many different people over the years and pushing through difficult circumstances formed bonds that will last a lifetime. Even years after the fact, I still receive notes from victims or their families, thanking me for my service. That gives me a huge level of satisfaction.

My years of SAR work have taught me a lot about life, death, and how uncertain things can be. I know all too well that, as beautiful as the mountains are, one can lose their life in them very quickly. And yet, after all that has passed, I am still intensely drawn to them. Thankfully, in spite of bearing witness to so much mayhem and tragedy, I've managed to maintain my sense of humor, as well.

Famed theologian Dr. Oswald Chambers once said:

We are inclined to be so mathematical and calculating that we look upon uncertainty as a bad thing . . . Certainty is the mark of the commonsense life; gracious uncertainty is the mark of the spiritual life. To be certain of God means that we are uncertain in all our ways, we do not know what a day may bring forth. This is generally said with a sigh of sadness; it should rather be an expression of breathless expectation!

Even with all that I've witnessed, I always go back to the high and wild places with exactly that: breathless expectation.

CHAPTER 9

Greater love has no one than this,
that he lay down his life for his friends.

John 15:13

June 27, 1998
Mammoth Lakes, California

L ife in the eastern high Sierra is extraordinary. Year-round,
there is always something to do. Whether it's adventure in the
backcountry or an event in town, we trip over pleasure every
time we turn around.

At the age of four, my son Paden attended his first motocross
and discovered a passion for motorcycles. Every June, Mammoth
Mountain hosts a ten-day-long motocross event on a local track
built by ski-area founder Dave McCoy and his crew. The track, set
amid towering pines, offers stunning vistas of the surrounding
peaks and is consistently touted by riders and spectators, alike, as
their favorite on the circuit. The Mammoth Mountain Motocross
competition was one event we were happy to make a tradition.

On June 27, 1998, Leah's brothers, Bruce and Mark, were
visiting from San Diego. They had been to plenty of motocross
races, but they found our venue stunning. We wandered the
entire track, taking in the peaks and vistas from both bright
sunshine and the comfort of the shaded forest.

Paden had just turned seven and had grown to love the vibe

of the place. Each year the smell of motorcycle exhaust combined with the powerful scent of pine brought smiles to our faces.

That morning we got off the shuttle bus from the parking area, and I sought out my good friend, Luke Schwarzkopf, who was in charge of track security. We were entering the beginning of the busiest time of the year for rescue calls, and I wanted to be able to get back to my vehicle quickly should a call come in. Luke assured me he would take care of it.

All morning, race after race, we sat mesmerized by these incredible young men flying through the air on 200-pound hunks of horsepower. Having done my share of trail riding, I could appreciate just how impressive these guys are. And they're tough as nails.

Just about every race, some rider took an absolute digger of a fall, one that would send the likes of me to the hospital. But not these guys. They bounced up, kicked the bike started again, and off they went. Paden was enthralled, and I secretly prayed he would never want to take up such a risky sport. I know. Funny thing for a rock and ice climber.

At 1:30 in the afternoon, my cell phone rang. It was Lt. Cole Hampton.

"How would you like to go climb a mountain?" Cole asked, already knowing the answer.

"You bet! What's the situation?" I responded, trying to block the noise of the screaming motorcycles flying by.

"Three backcountry skiers were hit by an avalanche high on the north face of Mt. Dana."

My mind whirled. Very quickly, I told the lieutenant where I was, and that I would respond from here. I told him I would contact him for more information once I reached my vehicle. I arranged for Leah to pick up Bruce, Mark and Paden then took off in a run to find Luke.

Thankfully, Luke was near the entry gate. He got on his radio and blocked all bus traffic. Then we raced towards the parking lot in his vehicle. Less than ten minutes after the call, I was in my truck and rolling.

On the phone, Lt. Hampton filled me in. The trio had hiked into the peak from the Tioga entry gate of Yosemite National Park earlier that morning. At around 9:00 a.m., they were struck by an avalanche and swept down the mountain. Fortunately, none of them was buried, but all were injured.

One of the three was able to hike and crawl for three and a half miles back to the park gate to make the report. The lieutenant also let me know that the Park Service would provide helicopter assistance and fly in one of their medics.

At 13,061 feet, Mt. Dana is the second highest peak in Yosemite National Park. In spite of its altitude, its proximity to the Tioga Pass road and the low-angles of its southern and western slopes make it a popular summit for hikers of all skill levels. Though Dana's southern and western slopes are tame, its wild side is its north face. Here the mountain offers the adventure of a classic ice couloir and fine, steep skiing.

I arrived at the Tioga gate at 2:20 p.m. Chris Benziger, the injured man who had managed to get out, sat in a nearby ambulance. The Deputy who had interviewed Chris filled me in, while I dressed for the mountains and assembled gear on my tailgate.

Chris and his two partners, Adam Bloom and Greg Silvi, were best friends from the Sonoma wine country. They were all experienced skiers, having skied together in the Swiss Alps over the years. The previous big winter had left these higher elevations still fat with skiable snow in spite of the summer temperatures. Chris, Adam and Greg had hiked in that morning with the intention of skiing one of the slopes on the north face, locally known as the "Solstice."

They had had an easy hike up the west ridge of the peak to the slope. When they reached the Solstice, they found their intended line of descent capped by a massive cornice of snow and ice that had formed when the wind raced over the mountain and dropped snow to freeze on the ledge. Hiking along the top of the cornice, they realized that it was actually in two sections, separated by a faint, vertical ridgeline. They were able to climb down this rocky outcrop to the slope below the cornice and click into their skis.

From a point just below the huge overhang of snow and blue ice, they began to ski down. A few minutes into their descent, the massive cornice released from the peak. The initial wind blast, caused by so much ice displacing the air as it fell, blew them from their feet. Tumbling blocks of ice and snow, some the size of cars, struck their bodies as they were pushed down the slope. Incredibly, the debris had blown them clear of the deposition zone, saving them from certain death in an icy burial. All of them were knocked unconscious.

When Chris came to, he realized one of his ankles was broken. He crawled to Adam, who had suffered a serious compound tibia/fibula fracture. Greg was the most seriously injured. His right knee had been shattered, and his chest was crushed. He was barely able to breathe, a sure sign of lung damage. He had also suffered a deep gash above his left eye.

Chris and Adam were both volunteer firemen back home and had some medical training. Spotting a small island of dry rock in the middle of the slope below, Chris managed to move both Adam and Greg to this location. With some of their gear, he applied a splint to Adam's leg then did the same for Greg.

Having done all he could for his companions, Chris set out to get help. Mostly sliding and crawling, Chris made the three-and-a-half mile hike out in three and a half hours.

Though I had never skied that particular slope, I had climbed the nearby couloir on many occasions, so I knew the lay of the land. With Chris' description of the area of rock he had moved the men to, I loaded rock climbing gear into my pack, should we need an anchor to lower them down the slope to a better landing zone. In the time it took the Deputy to fill me in, I had dressed for the altitude and stuffed seventy-five pounds of gear into my pack, along with food and water.

The Park Service helicopter was just returning from having

flown in their climbing ranger and paramedic, Keith Lober. I knew Keith from previous missions. His depth of knowledge and experience were top notch.

The chopper landed on the road next to my truck. As I climbed aboard, I told the Deputy I would be calling down our equipment and supply needs for additional team members to bring.

Minutes later we flew into the cirque, an amphitheater-shaped valley formed by a glacier pushing debris ahead of it and then receding. Very quickly we spotted the three men on the tiny island of rock. The pilot had dropped Keith off at the closest reasonable landing zone, about a quarter of a mile from the scene. After sizing up the situation from the air, I had the pilot set me down at that same spot.

In spite of now being at over 12,000 feet, the sun beat down relentlessly. It didn't take long before I was soaked in sweat. I made my way across the north face of the peak toward the scene, following in Keith's boot prints. As I crossed the debris path the avalanche had left behind, I was amazed by the size of the blocks of ice before me: clear blue chunks, some weighing thousands of pounds. I arrived at the scene at 3:10 p.m.

Keith was tending to Greg. I dropped my pack, greeted Adam, and assessed his injuries. Other than his severely broken lower leg, he was otherwise okay. Chris had done a good enough job on the splint, so I felt it was best to just leave it rather than cause him more pain applying a new one. He asked for some food, but I had to decline his request, knowing he would be in surgery soon. To his credit, and in spite of the terrible pain he was in, Adam realized how serious Greg's condition was and allowed me to leave him to assist Keith.

I quickly went over Greg's injuries with Keith and radioed a list of needs down to the base crew: oxygen, I.V. fluids, a sled litter and more rope. I also requested the Navy chopper from Fallon. The Park Service chopper had no winch capability. It was also too small for multiple victims, especially patients lying prone in a litter.

Greg fought for every breath and was in an incredible amount of pain. I grabbed his hand.

"Hey, you just keep fighting, okay? We're going to get you out of here; you just hold on."

He nodded and managed a faint smile, and in his eyes I saw an encouraging resolve.

As we waited for the next pair of team members to arrive, Keith and I discussed options for getting the men out of there. The Navy chopper would reach us one hour after they launched. Initially, I envisioned a winch-cable hoist from our location. The terrain was too steep for a landing.

Then, as I scanned the ridge above us, much to my horror I saw that only half the cornice had fallen. A massive section the size of two rail boxcars loomed above us. The percussion of hovering rotor blades could cause the cornice to release, and we were right in the run-out zone. Keith agreed.

Our only other option was to slide the men down to the base of the slope, about 600 feet below. Here the terrain was ideal for a landing. I called down to base and requested an additional sled litter.

I received a call back informing me that Dr. Curtis Schweizer, a local anesthesiologist who had been in the area when the event started, was down at base and willing to come in to assist. I had them put him on the chopper with some O2. Forty minutes later, Dr. Schweizer arrived and skillfully took over Greg's care.

While we waited for the next team, I scouted anchor possibilities for our rope system. The rock gear I had brought was useless, as the formation we were on was completely devoid of cracks that would accept my gear. With all the snow around us, our only choice for an anchor was what is known as a "dead-man."

A dead-man anchor is made by digging a trench in the snow, perpendicular to the fall line and deep into the firmer layer below. Then a log or piece of equipment is dropped into the trench with a long sling attached. The sling is brought to the surface, pointing towards the bottom of the slope. Then the dead-man is buried and packed down tight. The firmness of the snow holds the dead-man in place, allowing it to take the load.

The next team, comprised of Steve Case, one of my teammates, and Rich Bearwald, another Park Service ranger, arrived with additional ropes and a collapsible sled litter.

Steve and Rich dug a dead-man pit, and I went upslope and retrieved two of the skis strewn amongst the debris. With a sling around the skis, we buried the dead-man and, in short order, had our anchor ready to go.

A few minutes later team member Gary Guenther and paramedic Pete Levy arrived with more O2, I.V. fluids and an additional litter.

The Navy helo had launched but was still a ways out. Greg would definitely not be able to sit up in the chopper, so we knew he would have to wait for that bigger ship. In the meantime, we felt we should get Adam out with the Park Service bird.

We alerted the helo and loaded Adam for his ride down the mountain. With three 200-foot lines tied together, we clipped the system into the dead-man and put the litter on belay. With Adam aboard and Pete heading down with him, we sent him on his way. Ten minutes later, he was being assisted onto the waiting chopper.

The day was getting long, and Greg needed a hospital badly. It was now 5:00 in the afternoon, and the sun was getting lower in the sky. The last word from the Navy was that they were enroute, but we had received no ETA. Greg was doing better with the O2 and I.V. fluids coursing through him, but we were concerned that if there were an issue with the chopper, we would have to take him out on foot. I called back to base and requested that any additional team members should start hiking in, just in case. A few minutes later, a team of three began their ascent.

At 5:40, we finally heard my favorite sound on the planet: those thumping rotor blades echoing across the cirque. We'd already packaged up Greg in the second litter.

"Hey bud," I leaned in to him to say. "Your taxi is finally here!" He nodded in gracious approval.

With Dr. Schweizer along to assist, we sent the two of them down the slope, as the helo circled in and set down. Minutes later the litter was at the waiting chopper, and the crew aided Dr. Schweizer in loading Greg aboard. What a relief it was to see them go airborne.

Turning back the ground teams, we called in the Park Service bird, and two by two, descended the slope to catch a ride out. As the sun set behind the distant peaks, I got on the last flight out just after 7:00 p.m.

We debriefed over dinner in Lee Vining, and I walked into the house at 10:00, stinky and tired. The kids had long since gone to bed, but I sat up and told the tale to Leah and her brothers.

In every way, this had been another textbook rescue. We utilized the resources we had at our disposal and had a fine compliment of talented people respond. The help we received from Dr. Schweizer was invaluable. As usual, the Navy had come in and saved the day. And most importantly, in spite of a lot of objective danger, no one else was hurt.

The next morning, I drove over to the hospital to check on Chris, Adam and Greg. All of them had gone through surgery. Adam was in a cast and doing well. Chris was resting comfortably with his wife, Dawn, at his side. Greg's fiancée, Dulce, greeted me outside his room then led me in to see him. Along with his severely fractured knee, his crushed sternum had bruised his heart. Some ribs had broken, a lung had collapsed, and his head sported a gash.

Though Greg ended up with a series of surgeries to repair his knee over the next year, all three men went on to make full recoveries. And I'm happy to say, all three became good friends of mine and remain that way to this day. A few years after the accident, I guided the three of them on an ascent of the north ridge of Mt. Conness, just a few miles from where I first met them on that incredible day.

For my efforts in the rescue, I was awarded commendations from both the California State Assembly and the United States Congress. This is the only time I've ever been honored in this way, and it was completely humbling. Seeing these men go on to get married, have children, and live productive lives was all the thanks I'd ever want. To this day, those commendations hang in my home, reminding me of my three amazing friends.

Adam Bloom -- In spite of intense pain, just sucked it up so we could tend to his friend.

Greg Silvi -- Worked hard for each and every breath for hours on end, never giving in to the pain or fear.

And Chris Benziger -- Hobbled and crawled his way down the mountain, bearing excruciating pain to save his friends.

My closest friendships over the years have been forged in the fire of adversity, bound together in a combined strength of character and resilience to overcome impossible odds. These are those kind of men.

I'm quite confident that my angels were not alone that day. Many showed up in the form of dozens of dedicated teammates, park personnel, a volunteer doctor, and the best our nation has to offer in those valiant Navy crews. What a privilege it is to hang out with such extraordinary individuals.

CHAPTER 10

For I am convinced that neither death nor life,
neither angels nor demons,
neither the present nor the future,
nor any powers, neither height nor depth,
nor anything else in all creation,
will be able to separate us from the love of God
which is in Christ Jesus our Lord.

Romans 8:38-39

January 2, 1997
June Lake, California
3:20 a.m.

I made my way through the dark, quiet house, added a few logs
to the wood stove, then pulled open the window blinds.
Waterfalls poured off the eave as rain hammered on the roof. I
clicked the coffee maker on and headed for a hot shower.

Minutes later, with coffee in hand and bacon and eggs frying
on the stove, I contemplated my day. Leah and the kids had been
gone since the day after Christmas enjoying time with Leah's
family in San Diego. A busy work schedule had kept me home.
After ringing in the New Year alone, I longed for the hubbub of
them – the sound of their voices, the smell of their hair, their
warm hugs.

The rain only added to my misery. It had started on December
30th and came in a consistent deluge fueled by an El Nino

condition out in the Pacific. Though the season had started out with a decent snow pack, El Nino's Pineapple Express roared through the high Sierra from Hawaii, bringing rain that fell on all that snow as high as 12,000 feet. The ground was beyond saturated and water flowed abundantly throughout the county.

With the rain ruining any opportunity to climb or ski, all I had was work, and even that was now compromised. More than anything, I was concerned that my numerous job sites could be inundated by runoff.

With my belly full and at the first sign of daylight, I made my way to my truck to check things out. After an hour of puttering around to various jobs, I was confident that we were weathering the storm well so far, but with the amount of rain coming down, I'd have to keep on top of it. The creeks around town were flowing higher than I'd ever seen, and some homes in low-lying areas were suffering flood damage. It was clear this was no ordinary storm system.

Back at the house, I hung my wet jacket near the fire to dry, made more coffee and placed a call to Leah.

"How's it going down there?" I asked sipping and blowing my hot coffee.

"We've had a great time, but we're all anxious to get on the road and get home to see you."

"Well, hopefully you won't have any road issues with all this rain. It's still pouring here. Some homes down canyon have flooded out, but so far all is good here at the house, and the job sites are fairing well. I'll just keep checking on things throughout the day. You guys travel safe. See you this evening. I love you all."

"Love you too. Stay dry."

I called Doug, and we chatted for a while about the insane amount of rain. Then I got back in my truck to make the rounds once again. I was monitoring the Sheriff's frequency on the radio as I made my way between job sites. At 8:30, I heard Sheriff Paranick calling the dispatcher. This initially struck me as odd, because normally by this time of the morning, the Sheriff would be at the office and not out on the road.

Then I heard him request a page out for the SAR team to respond to a flood event in the little town of Walker, a full hour's drive north of my home. He stated that three persons were trapped in a cabin by rising flood waters at the Mountain Gate Lodge.

I quickly turned around and headed back to the house, just half a mile away. I had all of my rescue gear in my truck, but I grabbed extra clothing that I thought might come in handy. Back in the truck, I called dispatch and let them know I was responding.

As I drove, I tried to imagine the scene in my mind. Mountain Gate Lodge is a small, family-run resort with a series of rental cabins located along the banks of the Walker River at the north end of Walker Canyon. The river is known mostly for fishing during the season, and averages a flow rate of around 700 cubic feet per second.

During the winter months the river is a serene place of stark beauty, with beautiful slabs of ice that form along its banks. I knew the cabins were well back from the existing riverbed, so the fact that people were trapped in one of those cabins gave me a pretty good idea of how bad this situation might be.

Not long after hitting the road, I heard the Sheriff call dispatch again. He asked them to contact the Marine Base at Pickel Meadows and request their Swift Water rescue team. Over the years, the Marines at the Mountain Warfare Training Center were an invaluable resource when we needed extra manpower. I now had a better idea of how serious the situation was at Mountain Gate.

Forty minutes later, I arrived in Bridgeport, our county seat and location of the sheriff's office. There I received a radio call from Sgt. Turner. He requested that I not attempt any action at the lodge until additional SAR personnel were on scene. I still had twenty miles to go, and whether I could even make it to the lodge was in doubt.

A CalTrans roadblock had been set up on Highway 395 at the

north end of Bridgeport, and when I pulled up to the crew, I identified myself as a SAR team member responding to the call. They advised me that the road ahead through Walker Canyon was being compromised and that I would likely not make it through. They wished me luck and let me pass.

Five miles north of town, I encountered a one-hundred-yard stretch of highway that was completely covered by six inches of flowing water. The entire Bridgeport valley, normally wide-open cattle grazing land, was submerged. Only the roadway remained slightly above water, and now that was beginning to flood as well.

A few minutes later Sgt. Turner was on the radio to let all other responders know that CalTrans would not be letting any other personnel through. The only other way to the scene was a detour from Bridgeport out through Smith Valley, Nevada, then back over to 395 at Topaz Lake before heading south to Walker. It added an hour to their response time. I decided to continue on until it was obvious I could not make it through.

Ten miles ahead, I encountered another CalTrans worker and stopped to speak with him. I let him know I was responding to the rescue call at Mountain Gate. He informed me that the northbound lane I was traveling on was already gone in five places in the canyon. He advised me to travel as fast as possible on the southbound shoulder once I reached the canyon. He doubted I would make it through. I thanked him and raced on.

Minutes later, I arrived at the top of the canyon. As I crossed the bridge where the east and west forks meet, I couldn't believe my eyes. Normally the river was twenty feet below the bridge. Now a mere two feet separated the bridge from the roaring confluence.

Another mile down the canyon I came to the first section of missing roadway. A one-hundred-yard stretch of the northbound lane had fallen away, replaced by an angry torrent of raging, deadly water. I hugged the southbound shoulder and kept moving.

As I continued down canyon, the current in the river intensified with the drop in elevation, and the river widened from its normal fifty foot-width to, at times, over a hundred yards wide. I continued hugging the southbound shoulder as tightly as possible.

I passed additional sections of missing pavement, and seriously considered turning around before it was too late. I figured that, as a last resort, I could always abandon my truck and climb up the slope above the southbound lane.

A couple of miles from the lodge, I came upon yet another CalTrans truck and stopped to talk with the worker. Just beyond his truck, the north-and south-bound lanes were entirely gone. He told me he didn't know what I might find ahead, but was advising me that he was getting out and would not be coming back. I told him I was going for it and raced down the shoulder, hugging the mountainside.

I had always harbored a fear of fast-moving water, and this was as bad as it gets. The next couple of miles were a nerve-fraying journey of terror, knowing that going back was not an option. Ten minutes later, at 11:15 a.m., I arrived at Mountain Gate Lodge.

In a heavy downpour, I was met at the scene by Sheriff Paranick and Assistant Sheriff Terry Padilla. They briefed me on the situation. Over the noise of the pounding rain and raging river, I looked the two of them in the eye.

"Look," I said, matter-of-factly, "I'll rig ropes here all day long, but I am *not* getting in that water under any circumstance."

I put on additional rain gear, as well as a personal flotation device (PFD) and my harness, and attached a few slings and my mechanical ascenders to my harness.

A handful of firefighters and paramedics were there, as well as half-a-dozen Marines and a few spectators. The Marines informed me that, ironically, their Swift Water rescue team was out of the area on a training mission. The few that were there were not trained but available to help with whatever they could.

Here at the lodge, the canyon was about 150 yards wide. The highway was on the west side, with the river paralleling it on the east side, up against a steep mountainside. The resort was made up of thirteen structures, including three homes, a series of cabins, and a horse barn, nestled amongst towering cottonwood and pine trees. The building closest to the highway served as the front office of the resort and was the home of the lodge's owner as well. One of the medics mentioned that the rear deck of this house offered an excellent view of the situation.

We walked up to the front door through ankle-deep water, but the entire interior of the home was flooded. We passed a beautifully decorated Christmas tree engulfed in four feet of muddy water. We arrived on the rear deck, and I was able to see that the situation was deadly serious.

The previous night, the Forbes family, a husband and wife and their eighteen-month-old son, had rented a small cabin in the center of the resort, halfway between the highway and the riverbed. While they slept, the river jumped its banks and began coursing through the resort. By the time they awoke, they were cut off from escape.

Their tiny cabin was on a rapidly diminishing spot of high ground. Their SUV was parked on the upstream side of their cabin. Two more cabins and a small barn with two horses in it were above that. Just beyond all of these structures, the main body of the river raged past.

Between our spot on the deck and the Forbes' cabin a long, single story building was completely engulfed in angry floodwaters. The water was four feet deep and moving at thirty miles per hour. This structure was standing up to a tremendous amount of surge and appeared to be ready to fail.

Immediately downstream of our position on the deck were two more homes. The first was a single-story, with a two-story just downstream of it. I suggested we move and try to get a different perspective.

Back at the highway, Lt. Hampton had arrived with a large rubber raft. He asked me what I thought of the situation, and I suggested he come out to the deck to judge for himself. By this time, the water at the front of the house, which had only been ankle deep minutes before, rushed through our knees. We faced upstream to get through it safely.

Once on the deck, I explained to the lieutenant that I could rig a series of Tyrolean traverses from the deck using a few trees out in the river, but that it would be time consuming. We agreed that it probably would not make for an effective rescue. Lt. Hampton let me know that the Navy rescue chopper out of Fallon had been requested but was unable to fly with such a low cloud ceiling. We made our way back to the highway to wait for more SAR personnel.

Back at the highway a county front-end loader had arrived at Sheriff Paranick's request. They thought the loader might be able to cross the torrent to the family. I voiced my opposition to this plan straight away. The water was just too powerful even for the 50,000-pound tractor. Fortunately, the loader didn't get very far before it was pushed downstream as its front wheels reached the deeper water.

We briefly discussed using the raft to reach the family from upstream. I was also hoping to get to the barn to let out the two horses. But a series of barbed-wire fences and other obstacles made approaching from that direction simply impossible.

I briefly thought about Pete and his expertise at kayaking this kind of water. This was an event that he was made for. Before I could get too wrapped up in his memory, I pushed the thought out of my mind.

At 1:15 p.m., the rest of our team arrived, including two experienced swift-water personnel, Shawn Moats and Bob Feiner. Shawn and Bob got into wetsuits along with the Marines. Once Shawn was suited up, I took him out to the deck for a quick briefing. We didn't stay long. This building was starting to show signs of collapse, so we made it off limits.

I grabbed a bullhorn from our rescue truck, and Shawn, Bob and I made our way downstream to the two-story house to see if something could be worked from there. Standing in the lee of the house, we saw just how strongly the water was coursing between us and the Forbes' cabin.

A twenty-five-foot motorhome had been washed downstream and was pinned against a small stand of trees in the middle of the torrent. Muddy water washed up the high side of the RV, and cascaded down the other side. Large chunks of debris raced by including 200-foot-long pine trees and sections of steel highway guard rail. At one point, a 500-gallon propane tank raced by, spewing its foul-smelling contents.

With the bullhorn, I called out to the Forbes family and let them know we were working on a plan and would notify them when we were heading their way. They seemed calm given the situation and retreated back into their cabin to stay out of the torrential rain.

The three of us then made our way back to the single-story house just upstream and climbed on the roof, using a small apple tree near the front of the house. Though this building was surrounded by three feet of raging water, it offered the best location for mounting our rescue attempt.

About then, Lt. Hampton radioed in and let us know that the Navy had lifted off and were on the way. This was excellent news, but we knew we needed an alternate plan should the chopper not make it. Shawn put me in charge of rigging a rescue line. Somehow I needed to get a line across that river.

I went back to my truck and grabbed a pack of slings, carabiners, and 300 feet of static climbing rope. We had no line gun to shoot a rope across with, so I asked amongst the firefighters and medics if any of them had a compound bow. One of them did and raced off to his home in Walker to retrieve it.

Back on the roof, I anchored our end of the line to a large cottonwood tree growing up right next to the roof edge. Minutes later, I was joined by a few of the Marines, and the medic arrived with his compound bow. With the bullhorn, I called out to Mr. Forbes and explained our plan.

We tied a light five-millimeter line to the arrow and

attempted a shot. But the heavy rain had saturated the line, and it fell short of its target. I called back to the roadway and requested a fishing reel. Minutes later, a reel arrived and the shot was made perfectly.

With the fishing line tied to the five-millimeter nylon cord, Mr. Forbes hauled the heavier line across. Then we tied our static climbing rope onto the cord. I pre-rigged a knot in the end of the heavy line and attached a locking carabiner.

Mr. Forbes hauled the line across, and we talked him through how to simply run the rope around one of the large cottonwood trees adjacent to their cabin and clip the line off with the carabiner. In a few minutes, he had our line secure.

Back on our roof of the single-story house, I attached my ascenders to the cottonwood tree anchor and ran the line through them. With them holding the rope, we were able to pull the line as tight as possible. The ascenders held it taut.

The Marines brought the raft from the highway and managed to get to our roof through the rapidly rising waters. With the raft on the roof, I fastened two long slings to the bow of the boat and clipped them into our line stretching across the river. Our plan was to put four men in the raft. Using the line, they would pull themselves across the torrent to the Forbes's island.

The first forty feet of water from our position looked relatively manageable, as it was in the lee of the long building just upstream. But once past that building, the team would be subject to another fifty feet of extremely fast, debris-laden water. We tied a separate belay line to the boat so those of us on the roof could assist in pulling them back.

Since we hadn't heard from the chopper, we decided to implement our plan. Bob and three of the Marines loaded extra PFD's for the family, along with a few other pieces of gear. As they were getting ready, we noticed that the long building just upstream which was creating the eddy now had water running completely through the structure. The siding was actually blowing off as the water exited the building. Clearly, that building was not going to last much longer, and they would have to pass below it.

The four men in the raft began pulling their way across the water. Almost immediately after they reached the raging section, they lost control of the boat, and the current pulled it down and around a small tree, hanging it up. In spite of all their effort, they could not get the raft freed from the tree.

Utilizing our belay line from the roof, they were able to get out of the raft and make it back to the eddy in the lee of the long building. Just as they got to that spot, there was a sudden large cracking sound. A small storage shed exploded from the pressure of the water. In seconds, the entire structure and its contents were gone. It was now 3:00 p.m.

With this shed gone, a stronger surge of water now coursed between the house we were standing on and our four-man crew. Debris washed between them and us, making it difficult and dangerous for them to get back to the roof. Then suddenly, from just behind them, a large section of siding exploded off the long building, nearly taking them down. Things were going from bad to worse. The river was rising at an alarming rate now. If that long building failed, the four of them would be crushed and washed to their deaths. It was a desperate situation that called for a miracle.

My mind raced for a solution, something I could rig that would help those men. Suddenly, a powerful pain hit my ears, and I turned to see the Navy helicopter coming in to a hover over us. Our miracle had arrived. I choked back tears as all of us shouted our approval.

I radioed up to the chopper and told them to go after our four guys, who were presently in greater danger than the Forbes family. They agreed. With the bullhorn, we alerted the Forbes family to be ready to go in a few minutes.

The crew held the chopper in a hover and began the process of hauling Bob and the Marines out of the river with the winch cable. There were six of us on the roof: three Marines, one of the medics, Shawn and myself. It was time for us to make our escape.

From our vantage point we could see that the rest of the team on the highway were being forced to retreat. The highway was now flooded with knee deep, fast moving water. Things were getting ugly quick.

We agreed to move in two groups of three. Two Marines and the medic made their way down the little apple tree, which was now nearly engulfed in water. Shawn, David, the last of the Marines, and I watched as they battled the water. They moved downstream and made their way along the building, then carefully crossed the gap of raging water between the building we were on and the two-story house. The water was much deeper here and the current infinitely stronger.

Once they reached the second house, the three climbed onto a three-foot-high rock veneer that was part of the wall structure in an attempt to get out of the current. Clinging onto the siding boards, they traversed the wall to where a tree growing against the house blocked their path. At this point, they locked arms and waded out into the torrent.

Other team members watching from the highway were prepared with lines to throw to the men as they drew near. After a few close calls with debris in the water, the three managed to reach the thrown lines and were hauled to safety.

Now it was our turn. Shawn and David were in wetsuits and were relatively warm. I had been in storm gear that had long since soaked through. I'd been in the pouring rain, not to mention waist-deep water, off and on throughout the day. I was desperately cold. And I hate raging water.

We were all in agreement. We would go out the same way the previous crew had. Shawn climbed down the tree, followed closely by David. As I made my way off the roof and into the tree, I looked across the rooftop and saw my ascenders holding the river line. Not wanting to leave behind a few hundred dollars worth of gear, I climbed back onto the roof, released the rope, and clipped the ascenders to my harness.

I climbed down the apple tree into the icy water up to my

waist. It took my breath away. I followed Shawn and David, and we made our way to the treacherous gap of raging water between the houses and crossed safely to the next house. The water was rising so fast that the small rock veneer was now underwater, but we stood on it to get out of the current the same way the other group had.

Once to the tree, we saw that our fellow team members on the roadway had been forced farther back. It appeared unlikely they would be able to get a rope to us. Another eighteen-inch cedar tree stood against the torrent about twelve feet out from the house.

Shawn shouted out, "I'm gonna' go out to that tree, then try and catch a line from the team. You guys do the same."

David and I nodded in agreement.

Shawn let go of the house and made his way into the torrent, barely reaching the small eddy below the tree. Team members tossed lines, but they came up short. Shawn made his way a few feet beyond the tree and managed to snag a line. David and I watched as he was washed violently downstream, but he managed to hold the line and was hauled safely to the flooded roadway fifty feet away.

David relented and told me to go next. I cringed as I stepped off the rock veneer and back into the deep water. Facing upstream, I forced my frozen legs against the current. I barely managed to gain the tree. I wrapped my arms around it and held on with all I had. My hands were frozen.

Once again, the team tossed ropes toward me. Shawn was doing his best, but none of the lines got within ten feet of me. My boots were full of water and felt like anchors ready to take me straight down. I made up my mind that I was not going to commit to the water unless I had a line.

Suddenly, a large chunk of debris slammed into the tree, lodging just above my painfully frozen hands. With the debris creating a damn, a huge surge of water enveloped me as it roared past either side of the tree. All I could see to either side was muddy water. It was like being inside a wave. My instincts told me to climb.

I reached up for the first branch, but my hands were like claws, unable to grasp. I hooked it with the crook of my wrist, then the next branch with the other. Clawing my way, I scrambled out of the water.

Twelve feet away, David clung to the tree growing against the building. The desperate look on his face matched my own.

Above the roar of the torrent, I yelled, "Climb that tree and get on the roof!"

Without hesitation, he started up.

Once I was high enough in the tree to keep my feet out of the river, I became desperate for rest. Using one of the slings hanging from my harness, I tied myself off to the branches and slumped into a fetal position. I stuffed my hands down into my parka in hopes of getting some measure of warmth back into my frozen and aching fingers.

David had made it safely to the roof. He fought against uncontrollable shivering brought on by both the cold water and fear. For now, he was safe.

I looked across the river from my perch in the tree and saw that the helicopter had finished hoisting out Bob and the three Marines and was now winching up the Forbes family from their disintegrating island. I also saw that the rest of the SAR team on the highway were being forced out of the area by the rapidly growing deluge. I was starting to feel very much alone.

Darkness was rapidly approaching, and I knew the chopper must be running low on fuel. Could they stay in the air long enough to retrieve both David and me?

With the Forbes family safely aboard, the chopper flew off into the gathering darkness to take them to the evacuation center a few miles away. As it disappeared around the end of the canyon, I prayed it would return. The rising water chased me higher into the tree.

David had scrambled up the steep roof, and was clinging to

the rock chimney at the ridge. The first floor of the two-story house was now under water, and the entire building was creaking and groaning. Suddenly, a tremendous explosion of snapping wood and breaking glass assailed us. I watched in amazement as the long building disintegrated, the raging, muddy water washing it completely away in just a few brief seconds.

Once again, overworked adrenaline glands flushed my system with raw energy. I was desperate for a solution and secretly hoped David had some sort of answer to our predicament. I called out to him above the roar of the water and waved him down to the edge of the roof nearest me. As he approached, I saw by the look on his face that he was not going to be of much help. He also had no gear with him other than the life vest he was wearing over his wetsuit.

The tree I was in was twelve feet from the roof he was on - - too far for me to make it to him without some rope. I yelled for him to see if he could climb down off the roof and make his way back to the other house. If he could reach that rooftop, he could retrieve a section of our rope we had left behind. Just twenty feet of rope would allow me to get out of my tree and onto the roof with him.

David eased his way to the edge of the roof, but one look at the swirling, icy death below forced him back.

He yelled out to me, "I think I can get over to the other roof, but I don't think I can make it back!"

I begged him to give it a try, but he was adamant that it didn't look good. He turned from me and went back up to the chimney. I slumped back into my fetal position trying to ward off the dread coursing through my veins.

My mind raced for a solution, and the thought of swimming for it plagued me. I didn't want any part of being in that river anymore. The entire tree shuddered as if it would topple over at any moment as debris slammed into it.

I needed an alternate plan, should the helicopter not return. Climbing higher into the tree to keep out of the rising water, I realized that I was now high enough to reach out and grab a set of cables that ran past the tree and between power poles both up and downstream of my tree. Being in the construction industry, I knew these low wires were television and phone lines, with virtually no voltage, and they were supported by a braided, steel cable.

I began to see a plan: a Tyrolean traverse. I could reach out and clip one of my slings to the cable, release myself from the tree, then traverse the cable above the water to the downstream power pole, about fifty yards away. A few of my team members were only thirty feet from that pole.

My heart raced at the thought of a possible way out. But concern over the integrity of the cable, or where it was attached to the poles, or the poles themselves, gave me doubts. I knew the upstream pole had been subject to the raging water for the past eight hours. It might be ready to go, and if I added my weight I could find myself in the water, hopelessly attached to hundreds of feet of cable dragging me under.

Along with the uncertainty of the cable, if it did work and I got out, it did nothing to help David. Whether I could be of any help to him or not was in question, but I couldn't just leave him there to die.

David was standing on one of the three remaining buildings. The other ten had disintegrated before our eyes over the course of the day. If the building immediately upstream from him went, the house he was on would take the full force, and the trees would be his only hope. I decided that traversing the cable would be my last resort, should my tree start to go down.

Darkness began to fall. The water rose closer to my feet. Another loud explosion of splintering wood caused me to whirl around, as the barn with the two horses completely disintegrated. I watched in horror as the horses were washed to their deaths in an instant.

My body shivered uncontrollably as I began to resign myself to the same fate. As I hung in my harness, I closed my eyes, and my thoughts drifted to Leah and the kids. They were likely home from their drive from San Diego. I was glad that at least they were unaware of my predicament. Oh, how desperately I wanted to be in their arms.

As thoughts of leaving them behind swept over me, I finally gave in, and I wept uncontrollably from deep within my soul. Picturing my own death in the terrible waters swirling beneath my feet brought on a fear like I'd never known before.

Over the roar of the river and the pouring rain, with teeth chattering, I cried out to God, praying that He would surround my family and me with His love. I wept as I was reminded of all the things I'd left undone that I knew God had put on my heart to accomplish for my family. I prayed that I would have another chance, but if death were to be my fate, that it would be over quickly. I asked him to cover my family, then resigned myself to His will, completely broken and humbled by His awesome might

Then I heard it: the unmistakable thump-thump heart beat of rotor blades. Looking downstream, I saw the chopper come into view with all its lights on. Down on my chest inside my parka, my radio crackled to life.

Pulling it close to my ear, I heard Lt. Hampton tell the chopper, "There's a man on the roof and one in the tree."

The bird came into a hover directly above me, its powerful searchlight pointing straight down. I leaned away from the tree against my tie off to try and get my white helmet out from under the branches so they could see me. I strained to hear the radio as the chopper held their deafening hover forty feet above me. David stood against the rock chimney, waving his arms wildly.

The helo moved away a bit, and my radio crackled once again.

"We can get to the man on the roof, but the guy in the tree is directly under the high tension lines, and we can't get the winch cable to him."

My heart sank. I looked up and saw the power lines twenty feet directly above me.

My mind raced with options. I looked at the cable and thought of going for it. Then I looked at my harness, and my ascenders, and then I looked across to David.

I got on my radio and called the lieutenant, and he repeated his message, "The chopper says they can't do anything for you."

"The *hell* they can't!" I screamed into the radio, my mind whirring. "Tell them to get a rope to the Marine, and I'll worry about getting to the f****** rooftop!"

As the chopper circled, I called out to David and waved him closer to me. Screaming at the top of my lungs, I told him the chopper was going to lower a rope to him. He needed to tie one end of it to the chimney securely then bring the rest of the rope down to the edge of the roof. His eyes told me he understood my plan, and he went back up to the chimney.

From my perch I watched the helo enter a hover forty feet above David. With the spotlight shining down, I was now able to see that the house David was standing on was being shaken off its foundation.

The crew chief leaned out the open side door of the helo, and they lowered a bucket on the winch cable down to David. He retrieved the rope and set to tying it off. In short order he had the line secured and moved towards me with the rest of the line.

From my vantage I could see that the tree growing up against the house had a perfect crotch of branches about eye level with David.

"Throw the line through that crotch of branches and out to me!" I screamed.

Thankfully, the plan clicked with him and he made a perfect throw on his first try. God love those Marines.

I pulled the slack towards me until I felt the other end of the line tug against the chimney good and tight. Then I went to tie a knot in the rope, but my hands were useless. My fingers were so frozen, I could not get them to perform the task. Then I remembered the ascenders.

Careful not to drop them, I unclipped the ascenders from my harness and attached them to the rope. With the slings I'd used to tie myself off to the tree, I clipped my harness into the ascenders. Now I didn't need my hands; the ascenders would hold me securely to the rope. Without hesitation, I pulled all the slack out, slid the ascenders as far up the line as possible, and jumped.

David watched as I swung out of the tree, across the raging water, and slammed hard into the tree against the house. In the arc of the swing, I had dropped down low enough to where my legs landed in the river, the current pulling me horizontally away from the trees base. Just as I had done in the other tree, I clawed my way out of the river with the crook of my wrists, while David pulled on the line from above.

A couple of terrifying minutes later, I scratched my way up the tree and pulled onto the roof. I wrapped my arms around David and nearly squeezed the life out of him. With the building shaking under our feet, I yelled, "Let's get the hell out of here!"

We pulled up the rope and made our way to the chimney. Rescue Crewman Vince Wade was lowered on the winch cable, bringing a harness for David. As David got into the harness, I wasted no time hooking myself into the cable. Seconds later David was set to go. We got him clipped to the cable, gave a thumbs-up to the crew chief, and the two of us slowly rose out of that hell.

I wrapped my legs around his as we spun in the wind. Seconds later, the crew dragged the two of us through the door and onto the floor of the chopper. The cable was then sent back down and Wade was hauled up.

As the helo rose, I rolled over and looked towards the cockpit. The pilot looked back at me, and I couldn't believe my eyes. I blinked hard, thinking I was seeing the actress Meg Ryan. She smiled at me, then turned back to the control panel and steered us towards the evacuation center. I thought perhaps the hypothermia had finally gotten to my brain. The one thing I was certain of: I was out of that tree, and away from that deadly, churning scene of certain death.

Minutes later we landed in the baseball field at the

Community Center in Walker. The chopper powered down, and the rest of the team came out to assist us. My legs were not functioning well, and I needed assistance in getting into the Community Center, which was packed with people.

As we entered, a cheer went up, with everyone clapping. I was stripped of my sopping wet clothes and given a warm blanket to wrap up in. David was wrapped in a blanket as well, and we were led to a long table in the kitchen, where hot drinks and food were set before us. Sitting right next to me were the Forbes'.

Over the next hour, David and I recounted our story to those gathered 'round. As I spoke, I attempted to drink steaming coffee, but battled intense, violent fits of shivering as the cold deep inside my body worked its way out. Slowly, my body eased itself back to normal.

Once I regained some sense of normalcy, I got up and approached the Navy crew. Though I knew most of them, this pilot was new to me. She was Lt. Anne Wilson. Not only was she one badass brave chopper pilot, she was every bit as attractive as Meg Ryan.

As I had learned earlier in the day, her crew had been contacted by the Sheriff but were unable to fly because of the heavy rain and low clouds. However, they continued to monitor the satellite images from Fallon and finally saw a window of opportunity that got them to the Mammoth Airport. Landing there, they topped off the fuel and waited.

Listening to the Sheriff's frequency, they heard our situation growing worse over the course of the day and decided to try to get to us.

At great risk, Anne and her crew flew the helicopter at tree-top level for sixty miles, weaving through canyons and staying out of the clouds. Their timing was impeccable. Their bravery and skill saved nine lives, including my own.

By 8:00 p.m., we were warmed and fed and ready to go home. Thankfully, the team had been able to get into my truck with a slim-jim and rescue it from the flood waters. After spending such

a desperate couple of hours in the treetop, it seemed entirely odd
to be sitting in the warmth of the truck as I made my way through
Nevada and back to Bridgeport.

I arrived at the sheriff's office at 9:30 and thanked Sgt. Turner
and the staff for all the efforts on our behalf. When I finally
walked in the door at home just before midnight, Leah couldn't
believe her eyes. She took one look at me and said, "Uh, you've
gone grey."

One look in the mirror confirmed it. At 36 years old, and over
the course of one extraordinary day, I had grown much older.

Leah confided that she did get a phone call once they arrived
home letting her know that I was on a rescue in Walker Canyon.
Thankfully, the person who had called her did not give her the
desperate details, and, like every time before, she simply expected
me to walk in the door at some point. Over the course of the next
hour, I shared my experience, letting her know just how close I'd
come to death's door. Before falling asleep in each other's arms,
once again we thanked God for His amazing grace and angels of
mercy.

Three days later, I made my way back to the scene. Or better
yet, what was left of it. I couldn't believe my eyes. Of the thirteen
original buildings, only two remained, and only portions of those
at best. The single-story house we had worked off of had been
sheered in half, and the remaining section knocked off its
foundation.

The two-story house was off its foundation as well, with the
entire first floor packed tight to the ceiling with mud, rock and
other debris. Only the foundation of the long building remained.
The watercourse between us and the Forbes's tiny island was
now a twelve-foot-deep by sixty-foot-wide channel of rocks and
mud. Their cabin and the two adjacent cabins were gone. In fact,
their SUV was the only thing that remained, standing vertical
after being undermined, and falling front end first into the new
channel.

Strolling around in what just days earlier had been a scene of certain death was surreal. I took a seat on a boulder amongst the devastation and thought about the events of that day. Once again, I took stock of all the little things that happened -- things that had kept me alive.

Had I not put on my harness that morning, or climbed back up on the roof to retrieve my ascenders; had David not been on the roof to tie off the line, or the chopper not arrived. So many factors that added to the puzzle, piecing together an escape route. I am truly a blessed man.

In the months that followed, USGS reports indicated that the Walker River, normally flowing at around 700 cubic feet per second, had, on that day, come through Mountain Gate Lodge in excess of 14,000 cubic feet per second. An eight-mile stretch of U.S. Route 395 had been destroyed in the canyon. It would take over a year to repair it. Damage in the region exceeded $100,000,000, with scores of homes destroyed in the town of Walker. Incredibly, not one person lost their life.

Our rescue at Mountain Gate Lodge might best be described as a successful failure. A combination of amazing volunteers went up against overwhelming odds. We all made our share of mistakes, but, in the end, we produced a positive outcome without loss of life. To be certain, all of us learned an awful lot that day.

Weeks later, the sheriff sent my two teammates and me to Reno. There we trained on the Truckee River and became Swift Water certified rescuers. That training taught me so much. I am certain that, God forbid I am ever again in the same situation, my approach will be far different.

Over the next few years, and before she retired, I flew many missions with Lt. Wilson and her husband Bill, who was a pilot in the same unit. For their bravery and professionalism that day at Mountain Gate, Anne and her crew were awarded the Navy Helicopter Aircrew of the Year. I will forever be in debt to Anne and her crew for saving my life. God's angels showed up in the form of these five incredible people.

On that day visiting the scene after the flood, before I strolled back to my truck, I made my way over to the tree that for a few desperate hours was my only solace. The river had taken it away.

CHAPTER 11

Grandchildren are the crown of old men,
and the glory of sons is their fathers.

Proverbs 17:6

I find it compelling that when God gave Moses His "Ten Commandments" for all of us to live by, He did so on a mountaintop. I've been climbing mountains for most of my life. With each one, it has been the route along the way that taught me lessons, making the summit that much sweeter. Perhaps God wanted Moses and the rest of us to realize that it takes effort, discipline and commitment to obtain a certain goal, and He used the journey up a mountain as the crucible.

The rugged beauty of the mountains stirs powerful emotions in us all. Most of the best days of my life have come in the mountains. And, as you've read across the pages of this book, some of the worst days of my life have been lived in the mountains, as well. It's ironic that a place of such beauty that can set our spirit soaring can also bring death with terrible swiftness and brutal destruction.

Edward Whymper knew these truths all too well. Born in England in 1840, Whymper had a thirst for adventure, and the mountains of the Swiss Alps were his milieu. At the age of twenty-five, Whymper led a party of seven men to be the first to stand on the summit of the famed Matterhorn, near Zermatt, Switzerland. The hour they spent on the summit was one of joy and elation.

Minutes later, as the seven men descended while roped together, their most inexperienced team member lost his footing and fell onto the team member below him. The combined force of their fall pulled the next two off their feet. Above them, Whymper and the two remaining climbers braced for the impact, expecting to be pulled off their feet as well. Instead, the rope snapped.

Whymper was haunted by the scene for the rest of his life, writing:

> *Every night, do you understand, I see my comrades of the Matterhorn slipping on their backs, their arms outstretched, one after the other, in perfect order at equal distances — Croz the guide, first, then Hadow, then Hudson, and lastly Douglas. Yes, I shall always see them . . .*

The four men fell more than four thousand feet to their deaths.

For those of us who seek these high and lofty places, we do so with the knowledge passed down by those who went before us. Before he died at the age of seventy-one, Whymper penned the following words of wisdom:

> *Still, the last sad memory hovers round, and sometimes drifts across like floating mist, cutting off sunshine and chilling the remembrance of happier times. There have been joys too great to be described in words, and there have been griefs upon which I have not dared to dwell; and with these in mind I say: Climb if you will, but remember that courage and strength are naught without prudence, and that a momentary negligence may destroy the happiness of a lifetime. Do nothing in haste; look well to each step; and from the beginning think what may be the end.*

I've pondered those words often over the years, with each and every broken body I've rescued or shattered corpse that I have recovered. In spite of the danger, the lure of the mountains dwells deep within my soul. Those of us who have tasted the joy in the journey and the sweet elation of a summit are planning our next adventure as soon as we begin our descent. To a climber, the risk is calculated. And that risk is worth the reward.

To all who knew him, Matthew Greene was a calculating man. As a high school math teacher, detail and calculation were second nature to him. So when he arrived in Mammoth Lakes in late June of 2013, he was a man on a mission: to climb as much as possible before the start of another school year.

He had an aggressive agenda and was in the physical shape to pull it off. In spite of his attributes, however, Matthew was about to make a miscalculation that would change the trajectory of his life and those of his family and friends, forever. By the time I heard his name for the first time on July 30th, 2013, Matthew Greene was dead.

July 30, 2013
June Lake, California

I woke early to a literal pain in the neck. It radiated up into my head and throbbed from the back of my skull to an uncomfortable place behind my eyes. I gulped Advil and waited for my chiropractor's office to open. After a good wracking of snaps, crackles and pops, Dr. Craig told me to rest and ice my neck all day. Sounded fine to me. My cell phone rang as I walked out of his office.

"Hi Dean, Dan Watson here."

Dan Watson was the Chief of Police in Mammoth Lakes at the time.

"Good morning, Sir, how are you today?"

"Well, we have a bit of a situation. Thought you might be

interested."

Over the next thirty minutes, Chief Watson filled me in on what was known about Matthew Greene. That one phone call would profoundly affect my life.

Just weeks earlier, thirty-nine-year-old Matthew Greene had wrapped up another school year at Nazareth High School, in Nazareth, Pennsylvania. Eager to get out west, he loaded up his car with the necessities for a climbing vacation. He arrived in Mammoth Lakes on June 26th, setting up his tent at Shady Rest Campground on the edge of town. Two days later he met up with Pennsylvania friends, John and Jill Greco, and their young son, Anthony.

For the next ten days, John and Matt set to climbing a few of the local crags. They also managed to get on some alpine ice, including the famous V-Notch Couloir above the Palisade Glacier near the town of Big Pine.

The pair were using John's car to get around. Matthew's vehicle had been diagnosed with a blown head gasket upon his arrival in Mammoth. It would be stuck in the shop until replacement parts arrived.

On July 7th, John and Jill left Mammoth as planned. Between foot power and the free shuttle buses in Mammoth, Matthew managed to get around, keeping the Grecos posted on his exploits via text message. His plan was to be in Mammoth only until his car was ready, then head to Colorado to meet other friends for some climbing there.

On the 8th, he hiked out to the Minaret Range west of Mammoth and soloed Riegelhuth Minaret. It was a full-value day of hiking with easy climbing on less than ideal rock. The following day, he took a shuttle bus north up Tioga Pass to the entry of Yosemite National Park. From there, he hiked up to the north face of Mt. Dana and soloed the Dana couloir.

This information was helpful to me, for it spoke to Matthew's assessment of the level of risk he was willing to take while climbing solo and un-roped.

After resting in town on the 10th, he hiked back into the Minarets the following day and soloed a route on Clyde Minaret, the tallest and most famous spire in the Minaret group. Though the climbing on Clyde is well within Matthew's skill level, the rock is often loose and unpredictable. Once again, this information proved helpful in gauging just what kind of risk Matthew was willing to take alone.

Over the course of the next four days, Matthew took long day hikes and ascended local peaks, all while waiting for his car to be sprung from the shop. He continued to update John and Jill on his adventures.

On the 16th, records show Matthew Greene went to the Mammoth Lakes Library to use their internet. At some point during the day, he received a call from the auto mechanic, who informed Matthew that his car would be ready on the 18th. Back at the campground, he paid for two more nights, then called his parents in Pennsylvania and let them know the good news about his car. He told his father, "I'm going out for one more long day in the mountains tomorrow, then I'll head towards Colorado as soon as I get the car."

Matthew Greene was never heard from again. Ironically, the detail oriented, calculating mathematician never told a soul where he was headed on July 17th, 2013.

On the 21st, Mammoth Lakes Police received a call from the campground host at Shady Rest, alerting them to a possible missing person. When they arrived at Matthew's campsite, the officers found his tent undisturbed. His clothing and miscellaneous gear were stowed neatly in his tent. His food and cooking supplies were stashed in the steel bear box near the picnic table. Nothing was out of order in campsite #164.

Matthew's belongings were packed up and put in a locker at the campground. Without any missing person report on file, all Mammoth P.D. could do was make a report of the abandoned gear and leave it at that.

Back in Pennsylvania, Bob and Pat Greene grew concerned. They had left numerous messages for their son on his voicemail, all of which went unreturned. John and Jill had stopped hearing from Matthew as well, though all agreed that Matthew was spending time in the backcountry and was likely out of cell-phone range. Also, without his car, he was unable to charge his phone, so it might be dead. With these possibilities in mind, they continued to wait for Matthew to contact them.

On the 29th, Jill managed to reach the friends Matthew had intended to climb with in Colorado. He had never arrived. Jill immediately called the mechanic shop in Mammoth. The shop manager said that Matthew was told his car would be ready on the 18th. He had never picked it up. Jill called the Mammoth Lakes Police Department. Her heart sank when she was told that his campsite was declared abandoned a week prior. Matthew Greene was now officially a missing person.

Mammoth P.D. opened an investigation, starting with Matthew's car and gear, as well as information from the last to see him alive: John and Jill. John had stated that Matthew definitely had an interest in spending more time on glacier ice. At the time, the Sierra Nevada was in the midst of its third successive year of drought, with minimal snowpack the previous winter. Now, in the heat of summer, the alpine ice was scarce. John had mentioned that the two of them had discussed the glaciers located in the Ritter Range, which included the Minarets, where Matthew had already climbed.

An inventory of the gear left in both his car and his tent revealed the following were missing; a large pack, a pair of mountaineering boots, crampons, and an ice axe. He was likely wearing a pair of approach shoes, which are light like tennis shoes but shod with sticky rubber like a rock-climbing shoe. All of his foul weather gear and overnight equipment were left in his tent, so it was clear he was planning on just being out for the day as he had told his father.

One more important piece of evidence was found: his

backcountry guidebook. Matthew was known to tear out the pages of the guidebook for a given objective then paste them back into the book upon his return. The only pages missing were the two pages covering the Ritter Range.

The best tool any Search and Rescue team has at their disposal is information. In Matthew's case, the information that was known was simply too minimal. The missing guidebook pages were not enough.

In a normal scenario, the missing person's car is found parked at a trailhead, at least shrinking the search area down to that trail. If Matthew did go into the Ritter Range, he would have either taken the shuttle, hitchhiked, or walked to the trailhead.

Without any evidence to put him at a specific starting point, the sheriff's hands were tied. There would be no search effort mounted by the SAR team. A few SAR members did hike to the top of the prominent peaks in the Ritter Range to check summit registers. Matthew's name was not in them.

The weight of all this hit me hard. My mind wandered back to 1984 when Laura Bradbury went missing at Joshua Tree when I was in my twenties. I will never forget the look of dread on her parent's faces. Now, as a parent myself, I could only imagine what Matthew's family was enduring. Suddenly, my neck pain was insignificant. All I knew was that I needed to get involved on behalf of that family.

I tried to get into Matthew's head and put myself in his place. If I were stuck without a vehicle in Mammoth and intended to spend one more day bagging peaks and climbing on some good alpine ice, the Ritter Range would have been my choice. More specifically, I would want to knock off the two highest summits: Mt. Ritter and Banner Peak. I knew I could do that day physically, and, by all accounts, a bold day like that was well within Matthew's ability as well.

I called Doug and filled him in on the facts then asked if he was willing to go in with me to search.

"When do we leave?" he shot back.

I checked back in with Dr. Craig, whom I had been seeing every other day for the past week and a half.

"You have a pinched nerve at C5 due to stenosis," he said. "You need to ice it and rest a few weeks."

The next morning, August 11th, Doug and I shouldered our packs and made the twelve-mile hike into the Ritter Range. I gulped ibuprofen like Pez.

The Ritter Range is a fifteen-mile long by nine-mile wide spine of spires and peaks that runs north and south within the heart of the Sierra Nevada. This scenic locale is located within the Ansel Adams Wilderness Area, which encompasses over 230,000 acres of pristine wilderness. Bordered to the west by Yosemite National Park and Mammoth Lakes and all of Mono County to the east, the area is a coveted destination for backpackers, fishermen, and peak baggers.

For the average rock climber, the rock and its loose nature make the peaks and spires in the range less than desirable. Unlike the monolithic granite that makes Yosemite's walls so attractive to climb, the meta-volcanic rock in the Ritter Range is tantamount to climbing a stack of graham crackers. The area is arguably one of the most dangerous places to climb in the entire Sierra Nevada. Especially alone.

What the range lacks in vertical attractions, it makes up for in nearly incomparable scenic beauty. Shimmering lakes and sparkling creeks abound, and the jagged nature of the skyline provides even the most amateur of photographers the ability to nab quality pictures. It's simply one of those areas that any backpacker worth their salt would want to have on their resume.

Capping the north end of the range are its two high points: Mt. Ritter, at 13,157 feet, and its slightly lower neighbor to the north, Banner Peak, at 12,936 feet. Along with the eastern slope of the Minarets just to the south, these two peaks are home to the glaciers and snowfields that were, in all likelihood, Matthew's destination. Doug and I set our sights on searching the most significant glaciers around the two peaks.

It's hard enough to find a living person in the jumbled mass of stone that is the Ritter Range. Finding a body would prove to be all the more challenging, especially one that had been in the elements for nearly a month. Doug and I were veterans of many SAR events in this environment. Sadly, most of them were recoveries.

The elements in this environment alter a body dramatically. Within forty-eight hours, the average human body will shrink to half its size due to dehydration in the low humidity. Additional environmental conditions like wind, rain, and intense U.V. rays from incessant sun dramatically alter the scene. Animals can scatter remains over a vast area. Now, more than three weeks after the fact, we focused on finding Matthew's equipment. If we could do that, perhaps we would be fortunate enough to find whatever remained of his body.

From the start we knew what we were up against. This would be the ultimate needle in a haystack. The entire range is a jumbled mass of shattered rock with infinite nooks and crannies. Imagine trying to find one of your eyelashes in Disneyland. Those were the kind of odds we faced. On top of that, keep in mind that we weren't even sure Matthew had gone into this area. The task was, in a word, daunting.

Searching this kind of terrain is arduous. One must look for something that seems out of place from the landscape: color, a shape, a reflection, something blowing in the wind. Anything that seems like it doesn't belong amongst the consistent matrix of the mountainside must be investigated. It had been too long since Matthew disappeared to be led to the scene utilizing our sense of smell. What we were looking for, we were likely going to have to step on to find.

I search this type of terrain in micro blocks. Every fifty feet I stop and scan 360 degrees around my position, both near and far. Looking behind is important, since it would be easy to miss something from a certain angle or in a certain aspect of light.

It is slow, grueling, tedious work. Moving through loose

boulders of all shapes and sizes is exhausting, as the altitude above 11,000 feet wars against the body. But it is addictive, too. Having made so many "finds" in the past, there is that constant draw to see what's around that next corner in hopes that you'll spot what you're looking for.

For the next three days, Doug and I searched the glaciers and boulder fields along the eastern flank of both Banner Peak and Mt. Ritter. High on the southeast glacier of Mt. Ritter, I found a single bootlace frozen to the ice, but it did not belong to Matthew. After thirty miles and thousands of feet of elevation gain and loss with no sign of Matthew, we headed out of the backcountry. Before I reached home, I was planning my next search.

I was back at the chiropractor the next day.

"How's the rest and ice therapy working for you?" Dr. Craig asked.

"Uh ... well ... I did spend some time with the ice ... sorta'.'"

For the next half hour, the good doctor filled me in on just how serious the stenosis in my cervical spine could be if I didn't manage it properly.

"That's why I've got you, Doc ... to get me running again."

"Dean, I'm telling you right now, there could come a point where my treatment will not help if you don't mind my advice."

"I know ... you're right," I said, as he wracked my neck back into alignment.

"Just give it some time before you go back out ... and if you don't feel up to it, wait a little longer."

Back at home, with an ice pack in place, I pored over the map of the search zone. From where Doug and I camped on our last night of the search, we had a fine view of the vast glacier on the east face of the Minarets. It would be a tantalizing draw for a climber looking to get on some splendid ice. I decided that was going to be the area for my next search.

Taking Dr. Craig's advice, I gave my body ten days of rest. In all honesty, my neck still didn't feel "up to it," but summer was waning rapidly. Soon, the snows of winter would cover everything we were looking for.

On August 25th, I was back on trail with good friend and long-time climbing partner, John "Cupcake" McDonald. John and I had met back in the '80s while climbing in Joshua Tree. We'd lost touch for years, then, ironically, both of us had moved to Mammoth Lakes around the same time. John has an impressive resume of climbs, and during our years of climbing together, we forged a solid friendship. John and I also attended the same church, so I knew him as a man of great faith as well.

We were pressed for time, as bad weather was forecast to move into the area in three days. We raced in and set our base camp at Iceberg Lake on day one and searched around the lower areas of the cirque. The following morning we got an early start, searching a large, dangerous portion of the glacier and the cliff band below it.

We pushed ourselves hard, fighting an intense, incessant wind that preceded the incoming storm. Near the base of the glacier, we found a single glove. But alas, it obviously had been there for at least one winter so was clearly not anything belonging to Matthew. Near the end of the day, we packed up basecamp and started the ten-mile hike back out.

On the trail, the shadows grew long as the sun started to set. "Cup" was out ahead of me, leaving me alone with my thoughts. The fading daylight and sinking temperatures reminded me that, before long, Matthew's remains would be buried under a deep snow. A profound melancholy invaded me, taking my mind off my aching neck. As I walked, I prayed. Soon, my prayer became a conversation with a man I'd never met.

"Hey Matthew. I know that what remains of you is here, but you are long gone. Though we've never met, I feel as if I know you. You and I . . . we are drawn by a love for the high and wild places.

"There are a lot of people working to find where you left this earth. Whether that will ever be possible, I just don't know. In a way, I'm envious of you. You've left us in arguably one of the most precious spots on the planet.

"At the same time your family and friends miss you and would like to know the answers to their questions. I want to find those answers for them.

"I wish I had known you were in need of a partner. We could have had an incredible time together. I'm certain your energy would have dragged me up a peak with you. And, perhaps, mine would have brought you home."

As I neared my truck at the trailhead in the last light of day, I was spent. My neck ached, but the ache in my heart was infinitely more painful. For so many years, these stunning mountains that I play in and am privileged to call home have brought me joy. But I'd trade all of that for the life of Matthew Greene.

Six days later, I was in Los Angeles beginning a project for a client. Though I was 350 miles away, Matthew never left my thoughts. The only thing I was certain of was that finding his resting place would not be a sprint. It would be the ultimate marathon.

Along with my nagging neck pain, I developed an infection in one of my big toes after my search with Cup. In mid September, I had the toe nail surgically removed, which meant more down time. Good for my neck, but not for furthering the search before the arrival of winter.

Back at home, my beloved yellow Labrador retriever was in failing health. Cush had been a member of our family for the past ten and a half years, and the thought of losing him weighed heavily on my mind. Between being away from my family, feeling poorly, the poor health of my dog, and being so far away from the search, I battled depression. I used twelve-hour workdays to try and ward off the pain, loneliness, and dread.

By mid October, my foot was ready to be back on the trail. I looked at the calendar and watched the weather each day. On the 21st, Leah called.

"You should come home. I think we need to put Cush down."

I drove home immediately. When I walked in the door, Cush saw me and managed a single tail wag. Now I craved his normal mauling and the serious beating from that amazing tail. Lying on the floor next to him, I could see the love in his eyes. He desperately wanted to get up and romp around with me, but he was in pain.

We had suspected a cancer of some sort, but it came on so fast, the thought of getting his 102-pound frame into the car and putting him through an hour-long ride to the vet seemed more than cruel. He lived his whole life here at our beautiful June Lake home. We wanted his last hours to be here as well.

We slept with him on the floor that night and called the vet the following morning. Then I went out on our property, picked a quiet spot next to our creek, and dug his grave.

The following day was simply one of those autumn days that makes living in the eastern Sierra so extraordinary. The leaves of the aspens on our property burst with vibrant yellow and orange, and the maples blazed fire-engine red. The sun breathed subtle warmth into the crisp air. Leah and I sat on the lawn with Cush, stroking his sore body and letting him know how much we loved him. The vet arrived in the early afternoon.

Lying across our laps, Cush felt our touch and heard our voices as he moved on from this life. With him wrapped in a blanket, I laid him in his grave, and Leah and I said goodbye to our incredible friend. We stared at his empty bed all day, straining to even find words.

The following morning, I received an email from Bob and Pat Greene, asking me if I would call them. My emotions were worn pretty thin, and the thought of speaking to Matthew's grieving parents filled me with memories of telling Pete's Mom he was dead. Before I made the call, I decided I would simply be as honest as I could about Matthew's disappearance, and hopefully not say anything that would come across too harsh.

Within the first thirty seconds of that call, I knew I was speaking to two extraordinary people. They thanked me for my assistance in the case and asked lots of questions, to which I gave frank answers.

"Matthew is very strong and physically fit, Dean," Pat said. "He is experienced and knows how to deal with challenging situations. He's strong enough to crawl out of there if he has to."

I swallowed hard.

"Pat, I can assure you that I have seen climbers far more experienced than Matthew not make it out of the mountains.

"Right now, all the evidence tells me that he went into the Ritter Range. I'm confident that after this much time, he's not coming back alive."

Near the end of our ninety-minute conversation, Bob said, "Dean, we have retained an attorney here in Pennsylvania to help us obtain a declaration of death, so we can begin settling Matthew's affairs. Would you be willing to speak with her?"

"Of course, Bob. I'll help in any way I can."

After hanging up the phone, I knew I had made two incredible friends. I was completely humbled by the strength and character of these parents. The following day I drove back to LA and called the attorney. She explained that she was petitioning the Pennsylvania court for a hearing on the matter of Matthew's death. She thought an affidavit from me detailing the realities of the case would help the judge better understand the likelihood that Matthew was dead. In part, my affidavit stated:

> "Due to the nature of the terrain in which he entered, I am convinced that Matthew Greene suffered a fall that either killed him outright, or caused him injuries that rendered him immobile, and he died of exposure to the elements. In this alpine zone, the fittest of persons will only survive 3 to 5 days, even without an injury. Based on my experience and the facts stated herein, I am convinced that Matthew Greene has been deceased since July 21, 2013."

While their attorney petitioned the court for a hearing, Bob and I instigated a series of email exchanges. I let him know how deeply I regretted being away from the search and how badly I had hoped to find Matthew's resting spot before winter. He told me not to worry about it. He knew Matthew was gone and in a better place.

"If he's supposed to be found, it will happen," Bob consoled me.

With the first snows of fall, the search season came to a close. I was deeply saddened that we'd be faced with going through a long winter not knowing anything at all. On top of that, the reality of the remains going through a winter cycle was hard to bear. Gravity and melt cycles pull the snowpack downhill, a condition known as "snow creep." This action pushes the things we were looking for into smaller, tighter spots. Our desperately challenging search would get even more impossible.

As winter set in, my friendship with Bob Greene grew, and the emails turned to phone calls. One in particular jolted me out of my melancholy.

"Hey Dean, how's it going down there in LALA land?"

"Well, the work is challenging, and I enjoy that, but my mind is still out in those mountains," I confided.

"I know what you mean. We miss our boy. Ya' know, I'm thinking about coming out there next spring."

"Bob, I think that would be great. You and Pat can come up to Minaret Vista. It's a nice overlook that commands a fine view of the entire range. From there, you can see the search area where I believe Matthew rests."

"No, Dean. I don't think you understand. I want to come out there and search with you."

I hesitated for a moment.

"How old are you, Bob?"

"I'm 67".

"Do you do any hiking back there in Pennsylvania?"

"I usually go deer hunting one weekend a year."

"Uh huh. What kind of shape are you in?"

"Well, I could definitely stand to lose about forty pounds".

"Uh huh. You need to understand something, Bob. This terrain is unforgiving. Most of the search area is off trail and above 11,000 feet. The altitude alone will wear you into the ground. I'm in pretty good shape, and I get my butt kicked out there. Besides, the odds of finding anything at all are unfathomable."

Back and forth our conversation went, with me doing everything I could to convince Bob how bad an idea this was. I threw everything I could at him to talk him out of it.

"I'll tell you what, Bob. Here's the deal. You go over to Matthew's house and get one of his packs. Load it with forty-five pounds of stuff. Then you hike that pack all over rural Pennsylvania throughout the winter, get yourself strong, and try and lose some weight. Keep me posted on how it's going. Then we'll talk in the spring."

I hung up the phone having laid down the gauntlet. Smugly, I figured Bob would face reality. I was about to find out exactly who Bob Greene is, and what a father does for a son.

Over the course of one of the most brutal winters Pennsylvania had experienced in decades, Bob hiked that pack over hill and dale. He regularly reported in, sharing his experiences and his weight loss. I let him know that I had finally had an epidural in my neck and was feeling much better. Both of us were getting in shape.

On April 15, 2014, the family attorney called and told me that they managed to get a hearing, and, based on my affidavit, the judge declared Matthew deceased. With this painful step out of the way, they could begin to settle Matthew's affairs.

On May 8th, Bob arrived in Mammoth Lakes. He was forty pounds lighter, infinitely stronger and ready for an all-out assault on the Ritter Range. When we finally laid eyes on each other for the first time, there were no words. Just two fathers with tears in our eyes locked in an embrace forged by adversity.

From that day on, I started to learn all about Matthew Greene. Bob and I hiked, and in the evenings Bob talked about Matthew.

Born the second of four children, Matthew was a pleaser from the start. This easy-going, constantly happy toddler was given the nickname "Guy Smiley." As he grew, Matthew was drawn to the world of sports.

He hiked, biked and cross-country skied, but by the time he entered high school, he discovered his niche in running. Along with family and friends he hunted, fished, bowled, roller skated, and played soccer and baseball, but none of those activities filled his plate like running. Later, as an adult, Matthew would run the Boston Marathon a number of times.

"He saved his money," said his sister, Tiffany. "He bought his own TV and VCR and the first Nintendo. He could have hoarded them away and kept them to himself, but he allowed all of us to watch movies and play games with him."

When it came to sharing his love for the outdoors, Matthew dragged Tiffany along.

"He would take me fishing down at the dam where Dad worked. Matt always brought one of those Coleman lanterns along so we could fish until after dark.

"He took me hiking to the Glen once. He damn near killed me. It was all iced up and frozen over from winter, and he just booked up the mountain liked he always did. I was slipping and sliding all over the place trying to keep up, but I never could."

Matthew was a disciplined over-achiever who also excelled in the classroom. He graduated second in his high school class and spoke to his classmates at the commencement ceremony.

The time has come to fulfill our current goals and to set new ones to be conquered later. In our future travels and endeavors, no matter where they take us, we must not lose our youthful imaginations. We must not be too scared to take risks, and, most of all, we must live life to the fullest.

Matthew spent his first year of college at Clemson University in South Carolina then transferred to Penn State. He graduated with honors in 1995 and went on to secure a Master's Degree from Wilkes University.

For the next three years, Matthew taught at Twin Valley High School in Pennsylvania and did a brief stint as an investment counselor for a firm in Colorado. With his thirst for adventure as his guide, he joined the Peace Corps in 1998 and taught at Bema High School, in Morose Province, Papua, New Guinea.

While he was overseas, Matt gave Tiffany advice on a troublesome boyfriend.

"Any associations you have in your life can be lumped into one of these three categories," he wrote, "people who push you forward, people who drag you down, and people who do neither."

All of his letters to both family and friends included tales of adventure: hikes in the jungle and raging waterfalls on windswept mountains. He wrote about the dances he learned from the children in New Guinea and the funny names he created for them, like "The Poison Man Stiff-Leg Shimmy" and "The Pointy Toe No-No-No."

He wrote to friend Kathleen Timothy often and included a story of how he helped search for the body of a missing student.

"That story really got to me," Kathleen recalled. "It seemed exciting at the time, but now it brings up a feeling of sadness that I can't even begin to describe in words."

Back at home, Tiffany's admiration for her brother never waned.

"I wrote about Matt for my school papers. Anytime I had a paper due on someone I admired, or my idol, it was on Matt. I aspired to be like him."

In 2001, Matthew returned from the Peace Corps.

"I've always believed that his time in New Guinea is what led to his extreme independence," his father mused. "It closely resembled a military career, which helps a lot of young men mature."

Matthew worked as a substitute teacher and, in 2003 he took

a full-time position as a math teacher at Nazareth High School.

Matthew discovered climbing, and, like running, it quickly became a passion. He frequented a local climbing gym to stay in shape for what would become annual summertime climbing trips, ultimately leading him to Mammoth Lakes.

Now in early May 2014, two dads united in the High Sierra to find the remains of one father's child. I helped Bob find a rental condo to use as home base between searches. We sat around his kitchen table with mugs of steaming coffee, hunched over spread-out topo maps.

Together we identified the terrain to be searched. Bob was frustrated that the trails heading into the search area were still covered in snow.

I looked at him over my mug. "That's a good thing. You need to acclimatize to the altitude."

"While I'm gone," I said, indicating a few choice trailheads, "you can start by hiking lots of miles here in the front country, so your body will be ready for what the Ritter Range will throw at you."

I pointed Bob to every trail that was free of snow, and he wasted no time pounding them. Then I headed back to LA for work.

The family insisted Bob wear a SPOT device. These small transceivers utilize GPS technology and allow the wearer to be tracked on computer by anyone who has his device's code. As soon as a family member "logs on," a map appears on the screen, and a small flag shows Bob's location.

From my job site in LA, I watched Bob every day as he honed his physique. By the time the snow melted off, and I broke away from work to take him into the search zone for three days, Bob had logged over 400 miles of trail. But he was tired of just "feeding the mosquitos."

In late June, the trails were open and Bob was more than ready. Prior to his arrival in Mammoth, I had given him a list of gear he would need. Between scrounging in Matthew's stuff and buying a few things, he was well outfitted.

I had just come back from LA, and Bob and I met for breakfast in a restaurant in Mammoth. We ordered, and I took a few sips of steaming coffee. Bob put his elbows on the table with his hands folded as if in prayer and looked across the booth at me.

"What's the plan, Dean. Where do we start?"

"Well, as you know, I've spent a lot of time trying to get into Matthew's head."

"Here ya' go, gents." Maria set our breakfasts on the table and poured us more coffee. "Enjoy your breakfast." She turned and walked away, holding the coffee carafe high in one hand as she sashayed to the next booth.

I took a bite. "If I had been in his position, I would have headed for Ritter and Banner," I said, as I washed it down with a mouthful of coffee.

"But the Minaret glacier is awfully attractive as well. Cup and I didn't have time to search that area sufficiently. I'd love to finish that up."

"Sounds good to me. When do we leave?"

"I'll pick you up at 5:30 tomorrow morning. I've only got three days, so plan on food for that."

We talked and planned through the rest of breakfast. A few of Matthew's friends were arriving to help with the search, and Bob would likely hike over from our search area and join them once my time was up.

As I gathered and packed my gear that evening, I was nervous. For the first time in my SAR career, I would be searching for a deceased subject with a family member. How would he do emotionally? He seemed pretty fit, but how would it go once we hit the off-trail terrain? Would the higher elevation take him out? How would he react if we actually found Matthew's remains? I tossed and turned all night.

We shouldered our packs at the Agnew Meadows trailhead at 6:00 a.m. and hiked north towards our basecamp at Iceberg Lake. I was sizing Bob up from the start. Our destination was nearly eight and a half miles away and 1,400 vertical feet above us.

"You just hike at your own pace," Bob offered. "Don't worry about me."

"Oh, I will, Bob. I like to hike in an aerobic rhythm, and I have a long stride. But you hike at your own pace too."

For the first seven miles, he was right on my heels. At just over 9,000 feet, and with another mile and a half to go, the altitude was having a bit of an affect, and I began to worry. Bob lagged farther and farther behind. Just before cresting a ridge and losing sight of him, I stopped and sat down to wait. I didn't have to wait long.

"How're you doing?" I asked, as he arrived.

"That was a pretty good hill," he said breathing hard.

He looked around. "But wow! Look at this place!" he exclaimed, catching his breath, his eyes fixed on the glacier hanging on the cliff a few thousand feet above us.

He looked great, and he was eager to push the last bit to our basecamp at just under 10,000 feet. At 9:00 a.m. we reached our campsite next to Iceberg Lake -- the same spot Cup and I had used the previous fall. For the rest of the trip, I never had to wait on Bob again.

With camp established, we grabbed some food and our binoculars and found a comfortable spot along the lakeshore. Bob sat back and took it all in – the brutal beauty, the sparkling water, the rugged cliffs – not saying a word.

"This place is so spectacular," he finally muttered, "and so complicated. You weren't kidding when you said this is the ultimate needle in a haystack."

I let him absorb his own words as he peered through his binoculars at the shimmering glacier above.

"Yes it is, especially considering that from here, you are only seeing a tenth of the search area."

Bob didn't respond. He lowered the binoculars to take a bite of food, but his eyes never left the heights above. I believe I literally watched him make peace with the environment that had taken his son's life.

"I can see why my son would come to this place. This landscape screams adventure, and he lived for that."

Bob's eyes filled with tears. I looked away trying to hide my own. I'm normally the chatty type, but I sat quietly and let him drink in the landscape.

I found myself quietly praying, "Heavenly Father, thank you for this place. I pray that you would fill Bob with strength for this endeavor, that you would replace his pain with your perfect peace."

We sat just a few feet from each other, mostly in silence. I let the scenery speak to him. I wanted him to feel Matthew's spirit. Bob laid his binoculars on his thigh and looked up at the ridge. Then he looked at me.

"Ya' know, that kid never let any grass grow under his feet. He was always doing something -- or going somewhere."

"Sounds like my kind of guy."

Staring once again through his binoculars, Bob said, "Rosnau, you two would have gotten along great."

I smiled with the thought, "I'm quite certain of that, Bob, quite certain.

It was time to move on.

"You gonna' sit there feeding your face all day, or do you want to go do some searching?" I fired at Bob, choking back my emotions.

"Hell yes! Where are we going?" Bob shot back, jumping to his feet.

Pointing, I said, "Let's search this stretch of trees along the steep slope west of the lake. Then make our way over to the foot of the snowfield below the cliff bands and search that thoroughly." Bob nearly stepped on me as he headed for his pack.

This was another test. I wanted to see how Bob performed off-trail and how he handled the high-altitude heat and the relentless assault of the clouds of mosquitos. He passed with flying colors.

After a few hours, we reached the snowfield. The high afternoon sun turned it into a frying pan, with not a single bit of shade to be found. Keeping Bob in sight, I crossed the snowfield and headed for the cliff band on the opposite side, while Bob followed a stream of meltwater coursing down from the cliff above.

I reached the toe of the cliff band and searched the area, then decided to climb a few hundred feet to its top. I knew that above the cliff, Cecile Lake -- another popular camping spot for backpackers -- shimmered in the sun.

The cliff was low-angle, and the climbing was more of a careful hike than an actual climb. About a hundred feet up, I stopped in my tracks when I came across a water bottle in a small carrying pouch. I called down to Bob and told him to head towards me. Twenty minutes later, he arrived and ascended to me.

Both of us were unsure if Matthew had a bottle like this one. I took pictures, then put the bottle in my pack and continued climbing. Not fifty feet higher, I came across an old, rusty pocketknife. Clearly, it had been on the cliff for many years. We continued up.

Once we gained the ridge, I had a direct line of sight to the cell towers on top of Mammoth Mountain. I texted out pictures of the water bottle to a friend from the SAR team to try and find out if it might be Matthew's. It was not.

It was mid-afternoon under the sun's brutal rays. We hunkered down in the shade of a few small trees for some food and water. High above us, over the summit of the Minarets, storm clouds brewed. Within minutes, lightning crackled, and thunder rolled through the cirque. We headed for the trail leading from Cecile Lake and made our way back to our basecamp in light rain showers.

We cooked dinner as the remaining thunderclouds rolled across the sky. The heat and humidity brought out mosquitos with a vengeance. As we shared the last light of day, tears pooled in Bob's eyes.

"It's very strange," he said, almost under his breath, "being out here, knowing he's here somewhere, yet knowing I'll never see him again."

We sat in silence for a few moments.

"I can't even fathom it, Bob," I practically whispered. "As a father, all I can say is I admire you, and I'm in awe that you're out here."

"Well, I know you well enough already, Rosnau. If you were in my shoes, you'd be out here too."

"Yes, Sir." I swallowed the lump in my throat. "I sure would."

By 9:00 p.m., we'd had enough of the mosquitos. Bob said goodnight and headed for his tent. I had come with just a sleeping bag and bivy sack. It was too warm for me to sleep inside my bag, but the mosquitos were relentless. So I sweated inside the bivy while I listened to the bloodthirsty bugs attempt their assault.

The next morning dawned bright and clear. By 8:00 a.m. we were heading back up the steep slope above the snowfield, making our way to the high glacier. We gained the glacier at 10:00 a.m. and searched as we headed north. We wandered through the maze of boulders at the toe of the glacier. This was the most likely place for his body to collect had Matthew fallen on the steep ice.

Over the course of the day, we walked the entire eastern escarpment of the Minarets, hoping to find anything we could pin to Matthew. Exhausted, we arrived back at camp with nothing but fine pictures in our cameras. Our mosquito friends were waiting for us.

Once again, we took in the late afternoon light show while enjoying the peace and quiet of this sublime place. And just as I had the night before, I let the conversation come from Bob, as I prayed quietly to myself.

Bob eyed the alpine glow that bathed the towering cliffs above us. "I don't know how you do this, Rosnau."

"What do you mean?"

"Well, maybe the better way to put it is, '*Why* do you do this?'"

I made myself comfortable on a nearby rock.

"I guess the best way to answer that is to say, I can't *not* do it."

"That doesn't make a whole lot of sense. No one's making you come out here."

"Nope. You're right. Honestly, Bob, it just seems like the right thing to do. I'm convinced that God gives us all certain gifts in our lives -- things we're passionate about and that we can use to bless others.

"These mountains, they're a part of my life. I've spent a lot of time out here. I know this area well. I've been blessed with a few skills that make me useful in situations like this. It's . . . peas and carrots. It just feels right to me. It's what I was built to do."

Bob was quiet for a moment, digesting my words. "Yeah. I get that part. I guess what I'm curious about is . . . how do you deal with the hopelessness of it all?"

I took a long drink of water, thought for a second and looked at him.

"Perhaps on its face it looks that way. You're out here for the first time seeing the magnitude of what we're up against, and it does appear like an unsolvable puzzle.

"But I have the benefit of lots of previous searches where I've found what I was looking for. So each time I come out here," I waved at the mountains around us, "I do so with the mindset that I am going to find what I'm looking for . . . each and every time."

Bob looked down then raised his eyes to me.

"So, when we walk out of here tomorrow -- empty handed -- how will you deal with that?"

I leaned toward him.

"I won't walk out of here empty handed, Bob," I said quietly. "With each search, I'll at least find out where Matthew is *not*. That means on the next one, I'll be closer to where he *is*."

"Hmph. So, you don't get disappointed?"

I swallowed hard. My emotions crept into a knot in my throat.

"Of course I do." I sat back. "It's something I war against, but I can't let it win. It's far harder on me when I'm not out here.

"Working in LA right now . . . so far away from this place . . . it rips me up inside. But at least I can continue to work on it in my mind, wherever I am."

Bob thought quietly for a moment. Then he looked at me.

"I know my son would appreciate all you're doing."

" And I appreciate hearing that, Bob, but Matthew has gone from us and belongs to the ages now. I'm out here for you . . . for your family . . . and Matthew's friends. I couldn't live with myself if I didn't do something to help bring you all some closure."

Bob looked at me, and in the darkness, I saw the tears on his face. "What do you think the odds are? That he'll be found, I mean?"

I wiped at my own tears and looked directly in Bob's eyes. "It may not be me or you, but I'm certain someone will find what we're looking for. It could be tomorrow; it might not happen in our lifetime. But I believe it will happen."

Bob gazed back up at the cliff. "Considering this complicated terrain, that takes a lot of faith to say."

"I suppose. But it's also experience talking. Back in August of 2003, a man by the name of Fred Claassen left our county and hiked into the backcountry of northern Yosemite. He had left an extensive itinerary with his wife, including where he planned on setting his camps over his four-day trip. His intention was to record lightning and thunder on audio and video, so he willfully went during a forecasted thunderstorm period. When he failed to return, we had all this information from his wife to support our search.

"This was a guy who was known to stay on trail, so it seemed like it would be a relatively easy find, in spite of the fact that the search area was twenty-five square miles. We had literally hundreds of people searching. Multiple aircraft and dog teams, too. After six days, not a single clue was found, and the sheriff called off the search.

"I decided to continue searching. I checked all the off-trail areas along his route. Every summer, year after year, I searched.

Just over seven years after he went missing, some backpackers moving off trail came across his remains. The area where they found him was in my next planned search. So you see, it's just a matter of time."

Bob tilted his head toward me. "That really goes to show just how challenging all of this is. You guys had all that information, and it still took that long. We've got virtually nothing to go on."

"I'm convinced we have enough, Bob."

"Yeah, faith, right?"

"Ya' know, there's a lyric to a favorite song of mine that talks about faith. It says, 'To hear with my heart, to see with my soul, to be guided by a hand I cannot hold, to trust in a way that I cannot see, that's what faith must be.'

"That's the mindset I come out here with. I don't know what the day might bring, but I'm just gonna' do what I'm supposed to do."

"And look at this place," I said, straightening up and looking around. "I get to come out here. What a privilege!"

Bob stood next to me and looked up at the peaks before us. "You got that right, Rosnau. It's quite unbelievable. It's easy to see why Matthew came out here. He lived for stuff like this."

Bob turned and gave me a solid hug. "Thank you, my friend. I'll see you in the morning."

"Goodnight, Bob. We did good today. Sleep well."

As I crawled into my bivy, I realized that in a few short days, I'd grown a deep respect for a man I would have never known had he not suffered such a profound tragedy.

"Father God, thank you for this place, for my new friend, and for bearing Bob's pain and that of his family. May your peace come to us all."

We were greeted with a perfect morning, bright, crisp and clear. With coffee in us, we packed our gear and made ready to hit the trail. Bob would be heading up to Cecile Lake to meet Matthew's friends; I would make my way back to the trailhead.

I gave Bob some of my extra supplies. "You know where

you're going, right?"

"Yup. I'm good. You take care, Rosnau. Don't let LALA land get to ya'."

"Thank you, Bob. I'll keep in touch and let you know my schedule. It'll be good to get back out here with you."

"I look forward to it, my friend. Thank you for all you've done for my family."

I gave him a hug. "I'm sorry we had to meet under these circumstances, but I'm damn glad we did. Stay safe, Bob."

"You too. Go spend some time with your family." Bob turned with a smile and headed up the trail.

I must admit, it was painful to walk away from my fellow dad. I headed down the trail completely humbled by Bob's strength in the face of so much grief, grief that a father should never have to bear.

Just as it had with Cup, it wasn't long before the melancholy set in, and I found myself talking with and sometimes shouting out loud at Matthew once again.

"Hey Matt. Damn, you are hard to find! I sure wish you had left some information behind. *Damn it*! I absolutely *hate* this crap!

"But, I know exactly what drew you out here. It is so incredibly beautiful. You were as humbled by these mountains as I am, weren't you. I just wish we could have shared them together.

"I feel I know you so much better, now that I have met your dad. You were so lucky to have the father you had.

"Your father loves you very much. He's made an impression on me, Matthew. I know now where all the amazing things your friends and colleagues have told me about you came from. A father and mother who sowed themselves into you, taught you to fervently follow your dreams, to pour out on others, and to live a life of grace and integrity.

"I'm gonna' keep coming out here with your Dad. He's a great partner. I'm sure you're looking down on him with pride. And missing him, too.

"I thought I would have to take care of him, but, in spite of his grief, I believe he has found something special out here, Matthew. He has found what brought you here. And he is one with it. He fits in here, Matthew. The mountains that spoke to your soul, now speak to his.

"I'm privileged beyond belief to be able to call your dad my friend. We two dads are gonna' keep on keeping on, both with searching and with life.

"Climb on, Matthew."

Back at the beach in Los Angeles, the one-year anniversary of Matthew's disappearance came and went, as my little project continued to grow. What had originally been thought of as a four-month-long task was now at nearly a year, with no end in sight. Being away from my family and watching Bob's SPOT device as he continued searching alone, wore on me daily. When Bob had arrived in May, he let me know, "I'm giving it until the end of August, then I'm going back to my family."

In mid-July, Pat and Tiffany flew out from Pennsylvania and spent a week in Mammoth. Tiffany got out with Bob for some searching, which gave her a much better perspective on the challenges we were facing. And Pat got that amazing view of the region from Minaret Vista. It wasn't closure, but it helped them to see what drew Matthew to this sacred place.

When I was back in the mountains, Leah and I had them all over for dinner, along with Matthew's friends Viola Krouse; Patty King; and John, Jill and Anthony Greco. It was an intense time, with much laughter intermixed with plenty of tears.

"You know," I confided, "I truly believe that something good can come out of profound loss. Though I wish it were due to other circumstances, Leah and I could not be more blessed to know you all. For your friendship, we are truly grateful."

A few weeks later, on August 31, 2014, the same car that delayed Matthew in Mammoth precipitating his death, now carried Bob Greene away from his son's resting spot and back to his family in Pennsylvania. Behind him, this father left his footprints on over 800 miles of trail searching for his son.

Ironically, later in the fall, my schedule in LA freed up some, and I had time to come back and search before the arrival of another winter. Partners had become hard to come by. The brutal nature of the search terrain and the fact that we were not finding a single clue made it difficult for people to maintain any motivation to head back out.

In early October, a few other climber friends had searched while packing through the area. On their way out, one of them spotted what they thought might be a white backpack, high on a cliff side above one of the prominent glaciers between Ritter and Banner. They had run out of time to go back up and check it out. I drove straight home from LA and loaded my pack.

Some of the best days I've ever had in the mountains are days I've spent alone. That may sound ironic, considering Matthew's decision to solo cost him his life, but it can be done safely. One just has to use a different set of rules.

First and foremost, do not break the one rule that Matthew did: you must let someone know where you are going and when you'll be back. And that person has to be someone who will follow up and make the right calls, should you not show up on time.

Secondly, do not take risks that you might take with a partner. Discretion must be raised to a higher level. Hubris will get you killed.

Lastly, stick to your plan. If you do run into trouble, SAR personnel will be following your itinerary.

That being said, I still look at going solo into the mountains in two different ways. Going alone in the way I just described is kind of like playing Russian roulette. You're taking risk, but others know you're playing the game. And, if you do lose, at least everyone else knows where you lost.

In direct contrast, not telling anyone where you're going, in my humble opinion, is tantamount to suicide. Most suicides happen alone. Often, no one can explain why they happened. And most of all, the true victims of a suicide are the loved ones left behind.

As I headed into the Ritter Range in mid-October, I did so with my full itinerary in Leah's hands. Not a single mosquito was in sight as I headed away from the trailhead in thirty-degree weather. Fall colors surrounded me as I made my way up the trail, with my sights set on checking on that reported pack. The description fit Matthew's pack perfectly.

Three hours later, I made my basecamp above Ediza Lake, with a clear line of sight to the reported location of the pack. I pitched my tent and sat down with some food and my binoculars.

The area had been described perfectly. I immediately saw what did indeed appear to be a white and black pack on the cliff. I gulped food as my mind raced, and I had a conversation with myself.

"Should I race up there now? It's mid-day. It will take me two hours to get up there. If it is Matthew's pack, I'll have radio communications from that high on the peak, but it will be too late to get additional help to search for more evidence. That means coming back down here to base, then guiding additional personnel back up there tomorrow. That will burn more energy."

I decided to just take a short hike up onto the moraine -- the pile of rock and dirt left by a glacier when it receded -- at the foot of the peak to get a closer view with the binoculars, then climb the peak tomorrow.

After only fifteen minutes back on trail, I was glad I had decided to wait until the next day to head up there. My legs felt like lead, and my energy level was low. Still, my heart raced with the thought of perhaps closing this case.

Just before the face went into shadow, I scanned it with the binoculars from this closer vantage. More than ever, that looked like a pack. Back at my basecamp, I paced back and forth as the sun set behind the towering peaks above me.

As I crawled into the tent and my warm sleeping bag, I couldn't help but think of Bob. When he left for home, I felt at a loss. I had dearly hoped we would find something while he was

here and that I would have been able to spend more time with him. Truth is, I just missed
him.

I woke at 4:30 and set to brewing up coffee and making oatmeal. An hour later, with gear packed and ready, I began following the bobbing light of my headlamp up towards the peak. The air was a crisp twenty-four degrees, and, an hour later, I was greeted by the first rays of sunlight. It was a simply spectacular day.

I wasted no time racing up the peak, feeling full of energy and excitement. At 7:30, I reached the glacier. From this vantage, the object in question was blocked by a series of ledges on the cliff. I would have to get right up to it to see it.

The glacier was walk-able in my approach shoes, so I left my boots and crampons in my pack and carefully made my way up the ice. I had not brought an ice axe on this trip, relying only on my hiking poles for purchase on anything slippery. I never had any intention of getting on steeper ice on the trip.

At the top of the glacier lies the bergschrund -- a large crevasse that separates the glacier from the peak. I would have to find a safe way across it. The thought was not lost on me that Matthew's body may rest inside this awful spot. If he did lose his life in there, we'd never know.

Searching a bergschrund is virtually impossible, as they are shaped like a funnel. Most people who fall into one die of suffocation as they get wedged in as the funnel narrows deep inside the glacier. It would be all but impossible and incredibly dangerous for a rescuer to get into and out of such tight quarters. I estimated the depth of this one at eighty feet.

I found a place where the mouth of the bergschrund narrowed enough to where I could safely jump across. Minutes later, I scrambled up the ledges. There, lying all by itself on a sidewalk-sized ledge was a black and white rock the size of Matthew's pack.

I sat down. I realized then how easily I had let my mind

believe that this was it, the beginning of the end, only to have my hopes dashed. Admittedly, it hurt. I so badly wanted to see closure for the Greene's . . . and for myself.

I didn't sulk long. "Well Rosnau, you're all the way up here, you might as well do some good searching."

Across the cliff to the north was the standard ascent line: a twenty-foot-wide couloir that headed up for 500 feet to the saddle between the two peaks. The lower couple of hundred feet were choked with hard ice.

To the south, a narrow snow-filled couloir led from the glacier and along the bottom of the north face of Mt. Ritter. It rose up for nearly 1,000 feet to gain the same saddle a bit higher. Matthew had hauled ice-climbing equipment into the backcountry. This terrain would be in his eye. I made the decision to go check that couloir out.

I picked my way across the cliff face on ledges covered alternatively with loose rock and five inches of fresh snow. When I reached the couloir, it was entirely in the shade, and I put on additional clothing.

I was about 400 feet above the glacier and could not quite see to the bottom of the couloir. I decided to head down first, searching the couloir as far as the glacier, then make my way back up to the saddle, searching the upper half of the chute.

The lower I descended, the more challenging the terrain became. There was more and more loose rock and snow on the face, and it rapidly grew steeper. I continued on, growing concerned for my safety. I tried to stay out of the shade where there was infinitely more snow, and it was much colder. I allowed the sun/shade line to dictate my course of travel. Suddenly, I found myself in a desperate spot.

Just twenty-five feet below me, the gaping maw of the crevasse loomed. The opening was six-feet wide, and I could not see the bottom of the crevasse, only inky blackness, the mouth of a giant shark waiting to swallow me whole.

Slightly below me and to my right was a small ledge. If I could gain that ledge, I could get to a spot where the crevasse narrowed and cross it. Facing in to the cliff, I continued down. I suddenly found myself holding on tight with my right hand and extending my left foot down for some completely nebulous hold. I peered down into the crevasse, and the sirens went off in my head. To no one but myself I screamed out, "Rosnau!!! What the *hell* are you doing????"

I pulled myself back into a standing position and climbed as if that great shark were snapping at my heels. I couldn't get away from it fast enough. Just minutes later, I found myself 400 feet higher, where I had started my descent. Completely out of breath and mad as hell, I screamed out, "Damn it, Dean, you stupid ass!!!!! Make *better* decisions!!!!"

Once my heart rate calmed and I caught my breath, I decided I would search the remaining 600 feet of couloir above me to the saddle. From there, I would cross the saddle and descend the Banner couloir on the other side, then get back to the glacier.

I was happy to be back in the sun and climbing up instead of down. I regained my composure quickly, and my body warmed from the effort. Thirty minutes later, I reached the ridge. I was now at just over 12,000 feet.

Almost immediately, I spotted a hiking pole lying in the snow and rocks. Minutes later, I found a section of a fishing pole. It was clear that anything dropped while ascending the north face route on Mt. Ritter directly above me ended up in this spot. I stashed the items in my pack and moved on. I knew that neither of the items belonged to Matthew.

Off the saddle to the west a steep, wide, curving gully dove down to Catherine Lakes, 3000 feet below. The upper 1,000 feet were choked with snow and ice. This was clearly a spot where Matthew could have lost his life, and I desperately wanted to search it. But it was not on the itinerary that I had left with Leah.

Additionally, once I left the saddle to the west, I would lose all possibility of communication without line-of-sight to the radio repeaters on Mammoth Mountain. I had to make good decisions.

The gully would have to wait for another search -- and definitely one with a partner.

By the time I reached the north side of the saddle and the top of the descent route, I was nearly out of water. In spite of the cold air at this altitude, the sun blazed and UV rays baked me. I suddenly felt spent.

Knowing I would need to get into my crampons to descend the ice at the bottom of the couloir, I stopped at its top and switched into my ice boots. I gulped some food to try and get my system running better and drank water sparingly. Here at this altitude, the snow was still frozen. The nearest meltwater to refill my bottles was down at the toe of the glacier, 1000 feet below me.

I repacked my gear, setting my crampons just inside the top of my pack. Carefully, I navigated my descent of the steep chute. It was more of a controlled slide than a descent, as loose rock and dirt cascaded down as I went. I used my hiking poles to keep myself on my feet, all the while being cautious to stay out of a small stream of muddy ooze coursing down the center of the gully.

As I approached the ice below, I stopped about forty feet above it. I was 400 feet down from the saddle, with the toe of the glacier 600 feet below me. I needed to pick a reasonably safe spot to stop and put on my crampons. I spied a good looking spot just ten feet down and over to the right side of the couloir.

I took one step and went flying. The dirt that had been coming down the couloir had covered over the perfectly smooth, rock-hard blue ice.

I had been facing out, so I instinctively spun as I fell, attempting to dig my poles into the ice to try and arrest my fall, to no avail. My right hand popped off the poles, which I had been gripping with both hands, and I clawed at the ice with my bare hand as I rolled onto my right side. I scraped my boots as best as I could to slow myself and, after twenty-five feet, I managed to stop. Had I gone another ten feet, I would likely have shot to the bottom of the glacier, 600 feet below.

I was now in a bit of a pickle: prone on a forty-five-degree sheet of ice with no way to self-arrest should I start falling again. And my crampons were in my pack, which was on my back. I lay there for a few minutes to collect my thoughts. Make good decisions.

The edge of the ice where it met the rocky edge of the couloir was six feet away. I could try a desperate leap for that spot, but I was afraid my boots would shoot out from under me. If that happened, I'd be gone.

Looking down at my boots, I saw that a small pile of rock and dirt had collected there, jammed against the ice. This was likely what arrested my fall. I decided my only real option was to try and get to my feet on that tiny patch of grit and hope for the best.

Slowly, I stood. As I did, my water bottle shot out from off my pack. "Shit!" I yelled out. Thankfully, it lodged in a small melt hole just ten feet below me. Once I was on my feet facing upslope, I slowly removed my pack, keeping my lower body perfectly still. Carefully, I laid the pack across the ice at my feet. I was so thankful that I had moved my crampons to the very top of my pack while I was stopped up at the saddle.

I balanced gingerly on one foot and, all-too painfully, secured one crampon in place. I had banged up my ribs and hip pretty good in the fall. I was certain nothing was broken -- I had broken ribs before -- but I was hurting. Slowly, I attached the second crampon.

I breathed a little easier. With my pack back on, I carefully kicked the front points of my crampons into the ice and moved down to my water bottle. I was parched, and immediately drained the last few gulps. I alternated between front pointing and side-stepping, trying to rest my calves. As I was resting, I suddenly heard a noise coming from above me.

I looked up. A slough of mud, ice and rock was headed straight for me. The slide hit my feet with enough force to rock my nerves once again. "SHIT!!!!" I screamed.

I was now deeply regretting my decision not to bring an ice axe. Without one, I had no chance to self-arrest should I fall. In a calming voice, I said out loud, "Keep your shit together, Rosnau. Coolness will prevail."

I decided I needed to get off the ice as soon as possible. Another fifty feet below, was a spot that would allow me to cross the bergschrund. Then I could get onto the rock cliff face and easier, less risky terrain. Carefully, I front-pointed my way down, minding each step.

Once across the crevasse I was able to relax. I could see that I would need to descend about 100 feet of cliff to a point where I could cross back over the bergschrund and onto the lower angled ice of the glacier. I kept my crampons on, knowing I would be back on ice shortly.

I hadn't gone fifteen feet when my hand knocked a basketball-sized rock loose from the cliff. It took off, starting a sizable rockslide as it rocketed down the cliff. About fifty feet below me, the slide slammed into a boulder about half the size of my truck. When it did, that thing took off.

I watched in awe as this menagerie of rock and dirt slammed into the bergschrund, and then to my utter amazement, that giant boulder cleared the crevasse and shot down the glacier. Not knowing if anyone was on the talus below the glacier, I screamed a warning

"ROCK!!!!!! ROCK!!!!!!"

For what seemed like an eternity, I listened as that giant boulder went all the way down the glacier and then another 2000 feet down the talus to join the other rocks and debris in the moraine.

I turned my focus back to getting myself down, and quickly discovered two benefits of the slide. The rest of the cliff had been cleared of loose debris, and a dam of rocks that had been created at the lip of the bergschrund gave me a path across it. In minutes, I was standing on the relative safety of the glacier.

I made a beeline for the toe of the glacier 500 feet below, dropped my pack, and immediately pumped water into my water bottles. I downed a quart straight away and pumped two more.

Once I had water and a little food in me, I removed my boots and assessed my injuries. My right hip and right rib cage were severely scraped and bruised, the fingertips and nails of my right hand were ripped to shreds, and my right shoulder ached from trying to self-arrest with the hiking poles. All in all, I counted myself extremely lucky.

Putting my approach shoes back on, I decided to search the entire length of the toe of the glacier for any sign of Matthew. Two hours later, having covered the area well, I made my way off the mountain towards my basecamp, 2000 feet below.

Before I left the vicinity of the glacier, I looked up at where I had fallen. Very clearly I could see the line of my fall, and I snapped a few photos. I just shook my head, smiled, then prayed out loud, "Thank you Lord. Once again, your angels had me in the palm of their hand."

A few hours later, I arrived at basecamp, and I was hurting. I knew that come morning I would be bloody sore and stiff, so I made the decision to pack up my camp and head for my truck, ten miles away.

What had taken me three and a half hours coming in uphill the previous day, took me nearly five going out. I was trashed. My pack was now heavier with all of my gear, which did not bode well for my aching ribs and shoulder, and my feet were killing me from the very long day. I reached my truck just as the sun set behind the Ritter Range.

Back at home, I confessed to Leah that I had crossed the line and broken my own rules about going solo. I promised never to do that again. I sent off an email to Bob and Pat and let them know as well. Their much-deserved scolding told me everything I already knew. I had allowed the thought of the approaching winter to skew my judgment, and I had taken risks I never should have taken, especially for a deceased subject.

Just days later, I began making plans to go back in to search that ominous gully from the saddle down to Catherine Lake. No sooner had I secured a partner than the weather turned, covering the entire search zone with a season-ending blanket of deep snow. Matthew would have to rest in place for yet another winter.

While waiting for spring to arrive, I gave much thought to the search, poring over every piece of information time and time again. More than ever before, I became convinced that Matthew's goal was to climb both Banner Peak and Mt. Ritter, in that order. And because he had not signed in on either register, I believe he died while ascending Banner. From that point on, Banner would become my focal point for every search.

After spending the summer and fall months of 2015 in the search zone, Leah and I began to seriously discuss leaving the eastern Sierra. Having spent more than 27 years in the mountains, we were beginning to feel the need for change.

The harshness of the winters had worn her down, and I had become weary of dealing with it as well. Though our construction business had proved very successful, I felt I had achieved a pinnacle, and was ready to move on.

At the end of 2015, I laid my business down and retired. Six months later, after home-schooling our kids for 20 years, then teaching in the public school system, Leah retired as well. Weeks later, we did something we thought we'd never do. We packed up our belongings, and moved out of our beloved eastern Sierra. We settled on the central California coast, just ten minutes from Micah and her husband, TJ. I spent the rest of 2016 commuting to Mammoth to continue the search.

Admittedly, it seems profoundly strange to be so far away from Matthew's resting spot. Before, I was literally able to walk right out my door to begin searching. Now, I face a seven-hour drive to the trailhead.

This change has been challenging in many ways, but I've made peace with it. The bottom line is, I've done what's best for my family . . . something I've not always done through my life. Though I miss the daily dose of the mountains that I love, the perks of the change continue to show up. Just a week after moving, Micah and TJ announced the upcoming birth of our first grandchild.

Just two weeks ago, in stark contrast to searching for death, Abner Hosea Clark Russell arrived in our lives. Like the newness of spring and the upcoming search season, change has come, and life goes on.

Searching for Matthew Greene has become a deep introspection for me. Over the past four years of searching, I've found lots of pieces of equipment, but none of it belonged to Matthew. Admittedly, at times I've found my time alone in the search zone desperately lonely and overwhelmingly painful. But at the same time, I am always surrounded by the stark beauty that is the wilderness that never ceases to bring me great joy.

But more than that, I find a deep satisfaction in staying true to the things I've always held dear. In my youth, when my parents didn't want me to have anything to do with climbing, I resisted and pushed back. With copious obfuscation and outright lies, I managed to become a rock climber.

When I resisted college and was told I would never amount to anything, I followed my heart. My experiences in the vertical world and the skills I acquired in the mountains, led me to the world of SAR, allowing me a means of giving back to a community that I love. And my ability to craft sticks of wood into relatively useful things allowed me to provide for my family, and live a lifestyle that has been beyond our wildest dreams.

Working as a volunteer rescuer led our family to pursue similar things beyond our familiar world. In 2001, just after 9/11, we traveled to Quito, Ecuador and volunteered at For His Children, an orphanage run by dear friends Clark and Melinda Vaughn. The work there has the same feel that SAR does for me. Simply by taking the gifts we've been given, we are able to sow into the lives of perfect strangers for no other reason than it feels like the right thing to do.

While at the orphanage, we fell in love with a little 3 1/2 year-old girl named Marina, who eventually became our daughter. And Micah discovered her gift of working with children, which eventually led her to a training facility in Mozambique, Africa. There, she met another student who became her future husband.

High in the Ritter Range, I find myself alone once again after yet another tiring day in the search zone. Surrounded by beauty that few will ever get to see, I "listen" to the stillness, and I think about these things. It helps keep me focused and tuned into the fact that there is a bigger picture.

As the 2017 search season approaches, it looks as if it will be short one, as the Sierra was hit with a record amount of snowfall this past winter. If I get into the search area by the fourth anniversary of Matthew's disappearance on July 17th, I'll be lucky.

Some have called me "obsessed" with finding Matthew's resting place. I just can't see it that way. I simply believe that staying committed to the calling of my life validates the extraordinary path I've journeyed. Former British Prime Minister David Lloyd George once said, *"There is nothing so fatal to character as half-finished tasks."* Searching for Matthew Greene is just another bump in the road of a lifetime of years, with some hard-earned mileage.

And oh, what mileage it has been.

EPILOGUE

*Now faith is confidence in what we hope for
and assurance about what we do not see.*

Hebrews 11:1

When little Laura Bradbury disappeared in 1984, I was immediately drawn to the plight of her family. Their grief inspired me to get involved and changed my life forever. Just like Laura's, Matthew Greene's death is a profound tragedy. But there are lessons to be learned for all of us in the details that led to his death and what has transpired since then. I liken it to a well-thrown stone into a perfectly placid pond.

In this analogy, Matthew is the stone, which has disappeared into a place unknown. At the surface, the ripples go out from that place of disappearance. Those ripples are so many things: pain, sorrow, disbelief, tears, mystery, countless questions and unfathomable grief.

The ripples reach the shore, where those of us left behind are gathered, and it is there that we are united. We stare out, looking for what caused the tiny waves, but the origin is lost to us, out of our view. As the pond goes placid once again, we continue to look for the source of what united us. We are only certain of one thing: the source is out there . . . somewhere.

But just as the ripples cause pain, they also weave together those impacted by them. Complete strangers, brought together through a shared adversity.

I've had the privilege of not only coming to know the Greene family, but many of Matthew's friends, colleagues, and some of his past students, as well. Each one of these has shared a common belief: that the world lost an extraordinary man when Matthew disappeared. In his family, or while at work or play, Matthew inspired others with the way he lived his life. For those of us impacted by it, it was just painfully too short.

Matthew's own words to his high-school classmates resonate within my own life.

> In our future travels and endeavors, no matter where they take us, we must not lose our youthful imaginations. We must not be too scared to take risks, and, most of all, we must live life to the fullest.

I believe he met his goal.

Since he disappeared, I've often been asked my opinion about Matthew heading off on his own that fateful day. Admittedly, I'm always torn in my response. My SAR mindset would say, "Don't ever go alone." But as I stated earlier in this chapter, some of the most profoundly wondrous days I've had in the mountains, have been alone and un-roped.

We don't know how Matthew died, and likely never will know, even after we find his resting place. Clearly, he took a risk that didn't end well. But as far as I'm concerned, he only made one mistake that day: not leaving his itinerary with someone. I pray everyone who reads this locks that into their memory.

Theodore Roosevelt once said:

> It is not the critic that counts; not the man who points out how the strong man stumbles, or where the doer of deeds could have done them better. The credit belongs to the man who is actually in the arena, whose face is marred by dust and sweat and blood; who strives valiantly; who errs, who

comes short again and again, because there is no effort
without error or shortcoming; but who does actually strive
to do the deeds; who knows the great enthusiasms, the
great devotions; who spends himself in a worthy cause; who
at the best knows in the end the triumph of high
achievement, and who at the worst, if he fails, at least fails
while daring greatly, so that his place shall never be with
those cold and timid souls who neither know victory or
defeat.

Risk is a whole different subject, and certainly one of much debate. As you've read across these pages, you've seen that risk has been a part of my entire life. It's simply something I've always needed. Honestly, I'd rather not live life without a good measure of risk. Without it, I feel stale. I could never live a life of mediocrity.

At the same time, risk must be measured by each of us, and the cost must be counted. I know that once I started raising a family, I dialed the risk meter down a bit. After reading these adventures of mine, that statement might make you laugh. But again, all of us have varying ideas of what an actual risk is.

For me, I find myself much safer in all that the mountains have to throw at me than I do on the freeways of Southern California. And although I don't know how Matthew died, I'd rather go that way than wrapped up behind the wheel in a hunk of steel, glass and plastic.

Some might read my life's journeys and say I have a death wish. Nothing could be further from the truth. On the contrary, I desire to live life to the full measure. That's the attitude that put me on the seat of my brother's bike all those years ago, with feet dangling and the wind in my face.

Those same angels that may have drawn the "short straw" that day have been with me all my life. I've relied on them time and time again. And frankly, I believe they've enjoyed the ride.

On the cover of this book is a photo I took early one morning while searching for Matthew. The image is of the north face of Banner Peak after a savage night of wind and snow pounded my tent. I believe the stone in the bottom of that "placid pond" lies in this photo.

I'm committed to bringing Matthew home. My angels are ready and waiting.

Hiker Responsibility Code

• Become self reliant by learning about the terrain, conditions, local weather and your equipment before you start. Set realistic goals based on your experience, not someone else's.

• Tell someone where you are going, the trails you are hiking, when you will return, and your emergency plans. Be sure this person knows who to call when you fail to return on time.

• When you start as a group, hike as a group and end as a group. Pace your trip to the slowest person.

• Weather changes quickly in the mountains. Fatigue and unexpected conditions can also affect your hike. Know your limitations and when to postpone your hike. The mountains will be there another day.

• Even if you are headed out for just an hour, an injury, severe weather, or a wrong turn could become life threatening. Don't assume you will be rescued; know how to rescue yourself.

• **The International Distress Signal is three of anything**, i.e., three flashes of light, three whistle blasts, three lines tromped out in the snow, etcetera.

• Share this code with everyone.